....
About the Author
....

Jeff D. Opdyke has written about personal finance, family finance and the investment markets for *The Wall Street Journal* since 1993. For six years he wrote *The Wall Street Journal*'s nationally syndicated "Love & Money" column. He lives in Baton Rouge, Louisiana, with his wife, Amy, and their two children.

Piggybanking

PREPARING YOUR FINANCIAL LIFE FOR KIDS

· and ·

YOUR KIDS FOR A FINANCIAL LIFE

Jeff D. Opdyke

BUSINESS

HARPER
BUSINESS

Designed by Jennifer Ann Daddio / Bookmark Design & Media Inc.

Library of Congress Cataloging-in-Publication Data

Opdyke, Jeff D.
   Piggybanking: preparing your financial life for kids and your kids for a financial life / by Jeff D. Opdyke.
      p. cm.
   Includes index.
   Summary: "The must-have financial guide that shows couples how to afford kids, and how to teach them about money, from a longtime personal finance writer for the *Wall Street Journal*"—Provided by publisher.
   ISBN 978-0-06-135819-7
   1. Finance, Personal. 2. Children. I. Title.

   HG179.O6385 2010
   332.024—dc22
                                                          2009043807

10 11 12 13 14   OV/RRD   10 9 8 7 6 5 4 3 2

To Amy:

You've made all my successes possible.
I love you more than you know.

Contents

· ·

Introduction

· ·

It's a simple calculus, kids and money: From birth until college graduation, children consume dollars like they're chicken nuggets.

For those of us who aren't independently wealthy, that puts unrelenting pressure on the family pocketbook. The financial demands of raising a child require that money you otherwise might use to prepare for retirement, or to save for a nicer house, a sportier car or a swankier vacation, must, out of necessity, be earmarked for Lego sets and pediatric visits and school uniforms and Christmas toys and a college savings account and a minivan and a trip to Disneyland . . . and lots of, well, chicken nuggets. I'm not saying this to disparage kids. I have two of my own, and money is nothing in comparison to the happiness they bring me and my wife. Yet happiness does not negate the fact that the moment a child arrives—and, actually, many months before the arrival—your role as an adult changes in dramatic, profound ways. So, too, does your family's financial life.

Not only are you now on the hook for tens of thousands of dollars in costs over the next two decades, but you also have a new obligation to teach your children about money so that they grow into adults who are at home in the financial world and who have a healthy relationship with money. That might sound odd—"a healthy relationship with money"—but too many adults don't understand money and are so intimidated by finance that they routinely make a hash out of their personal financial lives. You, the parent, are the first and most crucial link in the learning process. Think about it: If you don't understand money or how to teach it to your children, how will they learn?

Thus, this book picks up where the first book in this series, *Financially Ever After*, left off. Where *Financially Ever After* laid the groundwork for couples learning to manage money and the money fights that inevitably arise, this book takes over when kids arrive. This is the parent's guide to the finances of childhood, both the monetary impacts on the pocketbook and the financial lessons that parents seek to impart through the years to their kids.

The first chapter is devoted singularly to preparing financially for a baby's arrival, and, for those parents who want Mom or Dad* to stay at home with the kids, how to think about ways to make a one-income lifestyle work.

The remaining chapters are aimed at the financial lessons

....

* (A quick disclosure: While I will routinely refer to "Mom and Dad" in these pages, that's simply for the sake of expedience—and because it is my personal frame of reference. I recognize, however, that in modern society other permutations are likely. Whatever your personal situation, the book remains equally relevant because, after all, kids are kids and money is money. Also, you will see that when talking about kids I routinely alternate between "he" and "she" or "son" and "daughter," rarely combining both in a single sentence. That's simply a function of a personal pet peeve: I despise the politically correct, yet utterly inelegant and verbose "he or she" sentence construction, such as "If he or she saves enough money, your son or daughter can afford to buy the toy.")

kids need to learn so that they have a solid grasp on money by the time they leave home and live their own lives. The chapters are split into natural divisions that track money's major categories: earning, spending, saving, investing, giving. There's also a final chapter titled "Learning" that covers the basics of what you need to know to save for and ultimately afford college costs for your child.

Why, you might wonder, is this book even necessary? Money, after all, is a seemingly simple technology. You've been spending it yourself since you were a kid, and you've been earning it at least a few years. What more is there to know about it, really? And what more do you really need to teach your kids that you don't already know yourself? Well, if statistics are any indicator, a lot.

In measuring how well twelfth graders understand the basics of personal finance, the nonprofit Jump$tart Coalition for Personal Financial Literacy found that a measly 10% could satisfactorily answer questions about personal finance. Many had no clue how to balance a checkbook. Overall, about half the students failed a test on basic personal-finance literacy.

Yet life as an adult clearly requires knowledge of personal finance. That doesn't mean kids need an MBA in security analysis or that you need to hire a financial advisor to tutor your preschooler. But kids obviously need better information to more effectively manage their own financial resources one day.

And that begins with Mom and Dad.

But parents are thinking about kids and money long before the day that they begin teaching their child about finances; the very idea of conception itself comes wrapped in one of the toughest questions couples grapple with: "Can we even afford to have a baby?"

I know many couples debate that question for years, continually putting off children until they feel they can afford it. Some never reach that point mentally because they never believe their finances are capable of handling the costs. Others end up pregnant unexpectedly and ultimately realize that the true answer to the question, "Can we afford to have a baby?" isn't really about affordability in the first place. It's about maturity, about moving past those dreams of material goods like the houses, cars and vacations you want and picking up in the trade-off the purest form of love and devotion you will ever know.

I learned this myself on October 12, 1996, a Saturday, at 7:47 A.M., when my first child, my son, popped into the world. For the nine months prior to that I was all but paralyzed by a generalized fear that my wife and I were simply ill-prepared for the financial obligations inherent in parenthood. Yes, we both had stable, secure jobs. We had a house and two cars that we could afford. We never went hungry, and we had the discretionary income that allowed us to eat out whenever the hunger pangs hit. We could afford some of life's niceties. In short, we weren't financially strapped. But that didn't change the fact that when my wife announced her pregnancy, my financial worries ballooned. And, given that I write about personal finance for a living, I worried about *everything* financial. What's this going to do to our budget? What won't we be able to afford? Do I need to start a college savings account now? Oh my God—college! How are we ever going to pay for that? And braces? And the doctor bills? How much is day care going to cost, and what do I have to cut from the budget to afford that? Do we need a bigger house? A safer car? And the questions kept on coming. "Do you realize how much money we're going to pay just for diapers?" I quizzed my wife with grave concern.

In truth, there's never a perfect time financially to have a baby. Couples who fall into the "We can't afford a baby now" trap typically find selfish motivations underneath if they're willing to examine their root concerns. They know a child will change their lifestyle and they don't want that—or, at least, one partner doesn't want that, fueling one of the most profound disagreements that can arise in a relationship. There's nothing necessarily wrong with such feelings. But if you're honest with yourself and your spouse about your real motivations, you will often come to realize that the money is just an excuse.

If I can tell you anything here, at the start of this book, it's this: The love you feel for your child, and the adoration that child expresses toward you, is worth every vacation you postpone, every restaurant meal you skip, every new sports car you never buy. Even the overused word "priceless" doesn't begin to capture the depth of the true affection you will feel. So . . . get over the money worries already.

Yes, your kid is going to put a big dent in your pocketbook. Yes, you're going to have to make sacrifices and hard decisions about spending and saving. You're going to have to do a better job of budgeting and learning to invest for your child's future. And you're going to have to teach your kids about all these same financial fundamentals so that they grow into adults who are confident about their own money skills.

The journey, though, is worth it.

So, let's begin . . .

The Rules of Kids & Money

· ·

Throughout these pages you'll find rules designed to help you in the sometimes inglorious, sometimes sublime task of teaching your child about money. Not to ruin the thrill of the hunt, but I present all of the rules here, at the outset. You can look upon this literally, a foreshadowing element to whet your appetite for what's to come. Or—and this is my true reason for including it—you can call upon this later; after you've consumed this book and you wish to refer to a particular rule; this cheat-sheet will lead you directly to the place you want to be without having to thumb through the pages trying to find what you seek.

Rule 1. Spending money happens only after you earn it. Page 34
Rule 2. When kids start asking parents to drive to Toys "R" Us to buy some plastic whatnot, the time has come to start thinking about an allowance. Page 38
Rule 3. The size of an allowance should not be so meager that your child is a pauper among peers, nor so generous that your child can easily afford all wants with little financial planning. Page 40

Rule 4. Good grades are expected, and helping around the house is simply the price of family life. Page 44

Rule 5. While 16 is generally the legal age of employment, encourage kids starting around age 13 to think of ways they can earn an income. Page 55

Rule 6. Guide and advise your kids about money, but don't dictate. Page 67

Rule 7. Failure to balance the monthly debit card bank account statement means losing access to the debit card for a week or more; failure to repay an entire month's credit card balance means the loss of the card until the balance is fully paid, plus one additional month. Page 90

Rule 8. Only 50% of the money put into a piggybank can be taken out to buy something. At least half must remain inside the pig. Page 101

Rule 9. Children should have the right to screw up financially so that they can learn from their mistakes. Page 109

Rule 10. When it comes to investing in stocks, kids should understand a company at such a basic level that they can draw a picture of the business model with a crayon. Page 130

Rule 11. You don't need to be wealthy to begin teaching your children about the stock market. Page 143

Rule 12. If a child's charitable interests lie outside your special interests, so be it. Page 169

Rule 13. Parents don't have to save every last dime a child will need for college expenses. You only have to save up to your ability or desire to pay. Page 174

Rule 14. One of the greatest gifts you can give your child is your own financial self-sufficiency when you're old. Page 176

Rule 15. At some point you have to tell your kids that the Bank of Mom & Dad is officially closed. Page 195

1

. . . .

Preparing

CAN YOU AFFORD KIDS?

If you believe in statistics, here are two that say volumes about children: The average middle-income family will, according to the United States Department of Agriculture, spend cumulatively between $184,000 and $270,000 raising a child through the first 17 years of life. Notice the age range—the Ag Department numbers clearly don't include the bills you'll pay for college. To that point, the College Board reports that the cost to educate a child for four years will, as of the 2008/09 academic year, add another $26,000 to $100,000 to the tally, depending on whether you're paying for a public or private university.

Whether those numbers tell the real story is debatable. The Ag Department methodology has some built-in flaws that effectively overstate the true cost of child rearing, and college costs can be mitigated by the university you select as well as the scholarships or grants your child receives. Those quibbles, though, sort of miss the point, which is this: Regardless of how you tally the numbers, deciding to procreate imposes a heavy financial burden on a family.

For many couples, or for just one partner, such costs are a primary reason not to have kids—at least not right now. They worry their finances aren't capable of covering the bills, and they routinely speak of waiting for a better moment, when their pocketbook is fatter or their income larger.

Unfortunately, the cost of raising a child doesn't shrink the longer you put it off. And your life isn't going to get any less expensive. Even if your salary goes up, you will undoubtedly find a way to incorporate that added income into your monthly spending, the result being that you're likely to feel just as pressed financially tomorrow as you do today.

So let's start this book by acknowledging that kids are expensive. They are. No question about it. But that's not a good reason not to expand your family. Yes, your financial life will be different. Not worse, mind you, just different. You will cut back on various daily expenses, largely those that are unnecessary, and you won't even miss them. You probably won't be able to take the same vacations you and your partner have grown accustomed to, and the roadster you drive, or the one you want, is probably out of the picture for now. You can rule out the loft downtown you hoped to buy because you're going to need more space, maybe even a place out in the suburbs where housing costs are cheaper. More dinners will be eaten at home, and your wardrobe will likely suffer as those dollars instead outfit your child. Whatever savings regimen you follow might suffer as well because you'll have pediatric bills and toys and darn near literally a ton of Happy Meals to buy. Your son will grow up wanting to play on a traveling sports team; your daughter will get involved with a dance squad; and your wallet will foot the bills for travel, hotels and all the pricey gear.

You not only face those costs of raising and educating your

offspring—those numbers the U.S. Ag Department and the College Board calculate—you also face all the preparatory costs of bringing a kid into the world to begin with, be that the medical bills or the bigger (read: costlier) house/apartment with enough space to handle an enlarged family. Then, after the kid arrives, money will become a central theme in your child's existence as the desire for consumer spending blossoms thanks to friends, family members, TV commercials and cartoons that play as poorly disguised product pitches for the latest toy/gaming fad. You will spend an inordinate amount of time dealing with an inordinate volume of spending requests. All the while, you will strive to teach the fundamentals of saving, spending and, at some point, donating to a worthy cause and maybe even investing for college, a first car or a first house.

All of that, then, is what "preparing" for parenthood is all about, and it also explains why so many would-be/wannabe parents are so freaked out at the thought of having a child. How, they rightly fret, am I going to afford a child based on my current income and expenses?

So let's begin by addressing that question: How *do* you budget for a baby?

Advanced Planning

Would you buy a car without first determining if your savings or monthly income can adequately cover the cost?

Planning for a kid is the same, only you can't really choose a less expensive model. Still, the point is the same: You have to do some advanced planning to prepare your finances for the costs that inevitably accompany parenthood.

The immediate costs to consider are all those expenses necessary in the first year—and they can be substantial. Carriages and cribs and clothes and baby food and the co-pays on doctor visits and prescriptions, and toys and diapers. Diapers . . . good goobily goo, the diapers you'll go through. Certainly, some of these purchases you'll avoid because family and friends will buy the items for you. Beyond the gifts, though, you are on the hook yourself for an ongoing litany of costs. Indeed, as the joke goes, "Parents are people who carry photos in their wallet—where their money used to be."

Pre-Arrival Expenses

Getting a handle on the costs before baby arrives, and preparing your budget, will help you better manage the expenses you will face. These expenses come in two broad categories: expenses before the baby's birth, and ongoing expenses that are necessary after your child joins the family. This list of items below represents for the most part the bulk of the pre-arrival expenses you have to consider. Some of these you might not need. Other costs might not be on this list, though you know they are mandatory, such as, say, replacing the family's two-seater car with a larger, safer model. Add those to your own list as needed. Do some research into the current prices for each of the items to come up with a budget for your pre-arrival expenses. This will help you know how much money you should save up for the initial outlays you'll need to afford:

- Creating a nursery: If you plan to redecorate a room, determine the costs for whatever it is you expect to do, from painting the walls to replacing the flooring.
  Projected budget: $ _____
- Nursery furniture: crib, mattress, dresser, changing table and whatever other furnishings you expect to buy.
  Projected budget: $ _____
- Bedding, receiving blankets.
  Projected budget: $ _____
- High chair, bouncy-swing, activity mat and other similar items.
  Projected budget: $ _____
- Baby dishes and infant spoons.
  Projected budget: $ _____
- Car seat and stroller.
  Projected budget: $ _____
- Baby toys.
  Projected budget: $ _____
- Baby bottles. You'll probably end up with about a dozen on hand, though good luck keeping tabs on the tops; they seem to disappear with the same regularity as Tupperware lids and the match to that lone sock in the laundry.
  Projected budget: $ _____
- Baby clothes. You'll be buying clothes over the course of the year as your child grows, but your initial inventory will include booties, gowns, footsie pajamas, pants, shirts, socks, hats and such.
  Projected budget: $ _____

- Maternity clothes for Mom.
  Projected budget: $ _____
- Diaper bag.
  Projected budget: $ _____
- A will. If you and your spouse don't have one, you really need one once a child enters your life. If tragedy strikes the two of you, you want clear directives in place on where your assets go, how they are to be managed for your child's future and who will be responsible for the care of your child. You really don't want the state making these decisions for you because they might not be the decisions you would have otherwise made. The costs here are those associated with a lawyer. Legal prices vary widely, though so, too, does quality. So, shop around and survey friends and family about which attorneys they recommend. You could rely on one of the online sites or out-of-the-box legal software that's available widely these days, but when it comes to something as important as who raises your children and manages whatever money you leave behind, I'd rather know that there's a professional lawyer standing behind the document, and not a toll-free customer service number.
  Projected budget: $ _____
- Miscellaneous expenses.
  Projected budget: $ _____

  TOTAL PRE-ARRIVAL BUDGET: $ _____

Ongoing Expenses

Once your child is here, the real costs kick in, since you'll have ongoing expenses for several years. Some expenses for the first year include:

- Diapers and baby wipes. Based on averages, newborns will go through roughly 75 diapers a week, while older babies (those between six months and a year) will consume about 40 a week. By similar logic, you'll be using a similar number of baby wipes each week, probably more. So calculate the cost of how many packages of diapers and wipes you'll go through in a month.
  Projected budget: $ _____
- Baby food/formula. Like diapers, you'll go through a number of jars and/or cans of food/formula. Depending on the size, you can go through about 20 jars of baby food a week and two or three cans of powdered formula.
  Projected budget: $ _____
- Co-pays. You will have a series of check-ups in the first year, as well as unexpected doctor visits when you freak out—and you will freak out—because your baby feels like she has a fever. You'll also have prescription costs. It's hard to price all of these medical costs, so just figure on co-pays for six doctor visits and a similar number of prescription co-pays.
  Projected budget: $ _____
- Baby pictures.
  Projected budget: $ _____

- Day care. If neither parent decides to stay at home with the child, you have to factor into your budget the cost of someone caring for your child, either in your home (expensive) or in a day-care facility (expensive, though generally less so).

  Projected budget: $ _____

- Date night: Though a baby is an all-consuming obsession, particularly in the first year, every parent needs to get away every once in a while for a bit of time with other grown-ups who don't speak in burps and babbles. Thus, budget a little money every month for the occasional night out.

  Projected budget: $ _____

- Life insurance. As with a will, if you don't already have a policy, you absolutely need one once you have kids. If something happens to either of you, you want the surviving spouse to have access to a sum of money necessary to provide for and educate your child (See related sidebar on page 10).

  Projected budget: $ _____

TOTAL ONGOING EXPENSES BUDGET: $_____ PER MONTH

Now, the biggest concern: How to pay for all of this?

Several items, particularly pre-arrival costs, you'll undoubtedly receive as gifts, so you can check those expenses off the list. With the remainder, the best option is to fit one or more items into your spending plan every month in the run-up to the birth.

So one month you allocate part of your discretionary income to the crib and high chair and bouncy-swing. The next month it's the car seat and stroller, and so on. These costs aren't a permanent strain on your family's monthly spending plan/budget. If you can afford to buy the items without thinking about the impact on your budget, great. If, however, several hundred dollars for baby furniture would hurt your finances for the month, then you'll need to spend time combing through your budget looking for costs you can cut or scale back that month or over several months. Set aside those savings so that you can afford the necessary pre-arrival expenses. This way your income is able to handle the costs without taking on debt.

With the ongoing expenses, including life insurance premiums, you need to tally up how much they're going to cost on a monthly basis. From there, you can begin to shape your budget to realistically reflect the impact of having a child. This will allow you to trim your expenses elsewhere, before you're forced to do so by the arrival of your offspring. Otherwise, you will be frustrated that your income seems incapable of affording your new life with an infant.

There's one particular cost you need to be aware of that couples often forget when planning their finances: maternity leave. Though "paid maternity leave" is commonplace in most developed countries, that's not widely true in the United States. Moms—or dads who take off for paternity leave—typically rely on vacation days, sick leave, personal days that they might have accrued, and sometimes disability payments. However, you probably haven't banked enough of those paid days off to cover the entire time you'll be out of the office. As such, parental leave is a cost that affects your budget because it represents income that won't be available for some period of time.

You can opt to structure your budget around that missing income, or, if that creates too much of a financial strain, you can aim to bank all or part of it over a period of months prior to your child's birth so that you have a cushion to draw upon later. Prior to baby's arrival, while you're both still working, consciously cut clearly extraneous purchases from your budget each month and stash that cash in a savings account. Your goal is to build a sum equal to whatever amount you'd otherwise go without. If Mom expects to spend three months on maternity leave and has just two weeks of vacation pay due her, then, to the degree that you're able, try to amass ten weeks of after-tax pay in your account.

When those paid days off finally evaporate, you'll tap into this account, and your budget will feel as if the income never went away. As a side note, make your savings work as hard as possible for you in the run-up to a maternity/paternity leave. By that I mean put your cash into a money-market or savings account at an online bank or a local credit union, both of which tend to offer the highest interest rates. This way, your money is earning as much as possible in the safest manner. That will make reaching your goal a little easier. You'll find a list of online banks through a simple Google search.

INSURING YOUR FAMILY'S FUTURE

Nobody particularly likes to contemplate their own demise, and that pretty well explains why people often avoid buying life insurance. If you're single and have obligations to no one

but yourself, disregarding the possibility of your own untimely death isn't such a big deal, since you won't be leaving behind people who rely on your income. And even if
you're married, not having life insurance isn't terribly bad
if your surviving spouse works and will be able to carry on
without feeling financially strapped.

But once a child joins the clan, your responsibilities
change dramatically. You suddenly have an obligation
that goes beyond you and your spouse. Now, you have the
responsibility for insuring this child's future. Forgoing it
can impose dreadful consequences on a surviving spouse
who's left to afford family life on a single income, assuming
that spouse has a career.

In the event a partner covered by an insurance policy
dies, the payout will help the survivor cover major costs,
including funeral costs, mortgage/housing, a child's education expenses or even some version of a retirement nest
egg—expenses that can be difficult if not impossible to
cover on a single salary.

To keep this really simple, shop for term life insurance.
Skip the whole life, universal life and variable life policies. Those policies have their place, but that place is generally associated with advanced financial planning. For
basic coverage insuring against an untimely death, term
life cannot be beat for affordability. You will always get
more coverage for the money, or to phrase it another way,
you will always pay less for the amount of coverage you
need. For instance, a $250,000 term life policy might
cost $30 to $50 a month, depending on your age, or

between \$360 and \$600 a year. The same coverage through a whole life policy can be five to ten times more expensive. To scale down a whole-life policy to the same price range means reducing the coverage far below that which your family needs.

Term life covers your need for a specified period of time, typically 20 or 30 years, though you can structure it however you wish. Whole life and the other types of so-called permanent life policies are generally in place for the duration of your life, so long as you continue to pay the premiums. However, the fact is that people generally don't need insurance for the entirety of their life. Insurance is designed to replace lost income when a breadwinner dies. Once you're no longer a breadwinner, and you no longer have costs to insure—such as a mortgage or college costs or raising a child—the need for insurance generally wanes.

How much coverage do you need? The industry's very general rule of thumb claims you need between five and seven times your annual, after-tax income (after-tax because life insurance benefits are not taxed, and you're only trying to replace the income you actually bring home). The more honest answer, however, is to tell you to consult an insurance or financial professional, preferably someone who offers independent analysis. Those who are tied to a particular firm have a vested interest in pitching products for that company.

If you want to do the work yourself, you can calculate your own insurance needs in one of two ways. Using the *income replacement* strategy, you determine how much income you need to replace over how many years. So, for instance, if your family needs to replace a $60,000 annual, after-tax income for, say, 15 years, your insurance needs are roughly $900,000. (Actually, it's a bit less, since you should calculate the present value of the money based on an assumed inflation rate, a fairly easy calculation for a spreadsheet. But if you don't want to muck with that, you're safe just multiplying the salary by the number of years your family might need to replace a lost income.) This method is best if you have no special needs to account for and few assets already saved to help afford life's various expenses.

The second method, the *financial needs* approach, is more robust—and slightly more complex—in that it requires you to think more specifically about what you need an insurance policy to cover. You first need to determine what those expenses are, including a child's college tuition, the family's annual living expenses, a mortgage payoff, the surviving spouse's retirement needs and possibly any special needs the family might have. After tallying up those costs, you need to subtract the assets you've already saved to help afford those costs. If you've already saved enough to pay for college, or if your house is paid for, then there's no reason to cover those costs with an insurance policy.

It's up to you to determine how much each expense will cost. You can gauge college costs, for instance, at www .troweprice.com, where a very useful calculator estimates future college costs at just about any school in the nation.

Mortgage payoff is as simple as calling your mortgage company to ask about the size of the remaining balance. Clearly, that sum will shrink every month as you continue to pay down the mortgage, so the insurance policy ultimately would cover more than the remaining balance, but that's fine; just consider it a sum the family can use for other purposes.

Ultimately, every family has its own insurance needs, some of which are highly individual, like, say, the need to provide funds for a special-needs child. Some families will not have a mortgage and, thus, no need to provide that coverage. As such, it's impossible to say you need a blanket five to seven times your income. Your actual need may be dramatically higher or substantially lower.

One other note: Don't buy a policy from just any old insurer that quotes the lowest rates. Insurers are rated (by Standard & Poor's, A. M. Best and Moody's Investors Service) based upon their financial health and claims-paying ability. The last thing you want to discover is that your insurer went belly up after you've paid for coverage for years, or, worse, when your family needs to file a claim.

Finally, new parents inevitably find their mailbox littered with solicitations from insurers offering insurance on your child. That's generally an unnecessary purchase. Insurance is at its core a mechanism for replacing lost income, and unless you've given birth to the next child star, your offspring probably isn't a source of income so much as a cost center. Thus, there's no income to replace and no need for insurance. The one real benefit of insuring a child comes if your child develops an ailment like, say, diabetes. Since insurance companies routinely deny coverage for an "existing condition," your child could find it costly or impossible to obtain coverage as an adult. However, if you purchased coverage prior to the malady's onset, your child should be able to continue paying for that coverage throughout life. Of course, the trick comes in guessing whether your child might develop some illness that would prompt an insurer to deny coverage.

One Income or Two?

THE FINANCES OF STAY-AT-HOME PARENTING

Many couples enter marriage having plotted a general course through life that presupposes a pair of working spouses. Some do this because of financial necessity. Others do so because they want the trappings of the upper-middle-class lifestyle that a dual income can help them to afford—private schooling for their kids, a home in a better suburb, nicer cars, travel, whatever. But then one day someone decides that leaping off the career path to stay at home with the kids is a better plan.

And so starts the tension—and the accompanying financial and emotional challenges.

One partner wanting to leave the workforce necessarily alters the financial dynamics of the family since the cash flowing into your coffers quickly dries up. Indeed, some of life's biggest financial decisions have already been made, and spending plans have been structured, around the family's two-barreled income. Suddenly one barrel's no longer firing, and all those decisions and plans and future expectations are in potential jeopardy. That's a situation clearly pregnant with potential conflict, especially if it's one that wasn't anticipated. Money is hard enough to deal with in the good times; throw in the stress that stems from an event like this, and it's enough to cause emotions to boil over.

Stereotypically, though not always, it's a wife who wants to stay at home and a husband who will continue working. And keeping with stereotypes, it's that husband who frequently bristles at the thought of the financial constraints imposed by losing a paycheck, and it's the wife who, in turn, bristles at her husband's seemingly selfish focus on money.

Problems emerge where these stereotypes fuel incorrect presumptions. A husband surprised by his wife's heretofore unannounced interest in quitting her job might presume—even if he doesn't say it in so many words—that she just wants to live a more relaxed life on the back of his daily toil. In reality, however, she might just want to provide a particular kind of life for her family, one in which she is home for the kids every day and can take care of the household chores without having to rely on cleaning services and prepackaged meals. On the other hand, a wife who wants to stay at home can mistake her husband's initial disdain for her idea for a frustrating preoccupation with what her salary can help him afford. If she probed deeper, however, she might find that he comes from a family where parents or grandparents struggled financially in retirement, and he is fearful of not having enough for the two of them to live on later.

Now certainly, I'm not implying that these stereotypes

always exist or that this issue always plays out in this manner. Sometimes it doesn't. Sometimes partners are on the same page and the transition to one paycheck from two progresses relatively smoothly. Other times . . . well, it's easy to see where conflicts can explode.

The only way you're going to know any of this, of course, is to refrain from reacting immediately and negatively if one spouse proposes leaving the workforce, or if the other spouse initially balks. Instead, talk about the pros and cons of a one-paycheck family and ask the $64,000—actually, the way-more-than-$64,000—question: Can we realistically lose a paycheck and still live the life we've come to know, or the life we want to know?

From that crucial question stems all of the related ones: Why should we do this? What does such a change mean to the family? Is it possible to make this work, and how? Can we afford our house or will we need to downscale? How will this impact our retirement planning? Our college savings? Will we be able to afford to go out to dinner or to the movies? How much will we have to scale back our vacations? What happens if the remaining breadwinner's job goes away—do we have enough money saved in that event?

For the spouse who wants to leave the workforce, the initial reaction to that big, overarching question—Can we realistically lose a paycheck?—is probably "yes." And they might ultimately be right. But, then again, maybe not. Listen to the concerns your partner raises about financial security, and, instead of instinctively defending your position, understand the reasons behind the concern. Then spend some time on your own considering actionable solutions that address those worries while still allowing you to achieve what you seek, too (we'll be looking at how to think about those solutions momentarily).

For the spouse who will continue to work, your initial reaction to that big, overarching question is probably "no." And you might ultimately be right. But, you might be wrong, too. Listen to your spouse's explanation of what he/she hopes to accomplish by no longer working, and instead of instinctively dishing up the obvious defense—we can't afford it—spend some time considering ways the family might be able to make this plan— or some version of it—work.

No matter what side you're on in this debate, to answer the fundamental question more accurately, you have to start with the money. So that's where we'll start.

HOW MUCH DOES YOUR LIFE COST?

Before you can begin to know if you can take the plunge and live on one income, you must know how much you are obligated to pay every month. Otherwise, you may realize too late that your life is too expensive for one paycheck, forcing you to make possibly rash decisions in quickly balancing the income and outflow. After all, if your expenses are $5,000 a month and the remaining paycheck only brings in $4,000 a month, living on one income clearly won't work without some financial restructuring.

So, make a list of your monthly expenses. And be honest about it. You can con your mind and your partner's into thinking that some alternate financial reality is accurate, but income and expenses never lie. Your family's financials will reveal the truth. In the upcoming exercise, you will find that not all of your expenses matter since some portion of your spending is obviously discretionary, and discretionary expenses will undoubtedly need to be axed to some degree to afford life on one income. But for now, include every item on your budget because both partners need to see these expenses so that they can make informed decisions about how to reduce costs in a way that will keep everyone happy. And that raises a key point: This budget examination process requires that you both be involved. You can't go into a one-income life with one partner sorely unhappy; that will breed contempt and frustration that will eat at the relationship over time. In this instance, "unhappy" could mean the working spouse feeling the family isn't placing enough emphasis on saving and investing for the future, or it could mean the stay-at-home spouse resenting being forced to relinquish every expense important to her (or his) life.

In practical terms, the breadwinner who will remain in the workforce needs to recognize that the stay-at-home spouse, though not earning a paycheck, has the same claim to the family's money and is entitled to spend some of it on discretionary wants. Likewise, the childrearer looking to leave the workforce needs to understand that—due to the financial impact such a decision has on the family—making the new life work may require some large trade-offs, including downsizing a house, changing a child's schooling or, maybe, agreeing to work part-time to generate necessary income. If you're the spouse who wants to stay at home, are you willing to make those kinds of trade-offs?

Let's start figuring out if life on one income will work:

Step 1: Tally your fixed costs. How much do the mandatory expenses in your life cost? This is a good spot to shamelessly plug my previous book, *Financially Ever After.* Along with helping couples manage the communication challenges of sharing a financial life together, it details all that couples need to know to manage their finances more effectively, including building user-friendly budgets, for which tallying your fixed costs is a key component.

These costs include all those monthly costs that you cannot escape, such as rent or mortgage payments; property taxes, if they're not included in your mortgage payment; car loans or leases and the gas to fuel the vehicle; other transportation costs such as subway or ferry passes necessary to get to and from work; premiums for health, auto, home and life insurance; utilities; food; and student loans or current educational costs for your children (don't include educational savings; you can reinstate that later. Moreover, kids will have plenty of opportunities to pursue grants, scholarships and student loans to afford college, or to work their way through school if necessary—but more on of all this in a later chapter).

From month to month, some of these costs are variable, not fixed, such as food, utilities and gasoline, among others. They are, nevertheless, "fixed" in the sense that you must spend some amount of money on them each month to live your life. Use the highest monthly sum over the past year so that you're analyzing your budget based on what you're likely to face in a given month.

By the way, you'll notice that the list of fixed expenses doesn't include a component for savings. That's not an oversight. Nor is it to imply that savings is unimportant in this exercise. To the contrary, saving is exceedingly important in every phase of your life. Moreover, before you begin to implement a one-income plan, you should build as robust a savings account as you possibly can to help offset the soon-to-be absent paycheck and to bolster the family's ability to withstand any financial crisis/hardship that might emerge, but more on all of that in a moment. The reality for most families is that once you do become a one-income household, your ability to save will likely be compromised. This means, of course, you will have to save a larger amount of cash later in life, once your kids are grown and you can redirect money to your needs rather than paying for your kids' needs. That could potentially curtail your lifestyle in the future. But that's just the trade-off the family has to consider when you're talking about giving up a paycheck.

The good news is that once the kids are grown, the stay-at-home parent has an opportunity to return to work and restart that savings regimen. Also, because you've structured your life for years around one income, and because the costs imposed by your kids are winding down, all or a significant portion of the paycheck earned by the person returning to work can be banked, fattening the savings and retirement accounts relatively quickly.

Step 2: Subtract these cumulative fixed costs from the monthly take-home pay earned by the one who will continue to work. This is your discretionary income in a one-salary environment.

If the result of that simple math is a positive number, your fixed expenses as calculated in Step 1 are less than your monthly one-income paycheck. Go ahead and skip to Step 3.

If, however, you get a negative number, your family's fixed costs already exceed what will be a single income, even before you account for all those discretionary expenses in your life, like restaurant meals, travel, the iTunes purchases and the DVD rentals.

If this is the case, you already need to find a way to curtail costs.

Instead of nickel-and-diming yourself on small-ticket items, you can start most efficiently by realizing that the biggest bang for the buck comes from some of the biggest expenses: your housing and transportation costs.

Renters: You might consider a less expensive rental property. Homeowners: You might consider refinancing a mortgage, a step that can trim a couple hundred dollars off a monthly mortgage payment depending on where interest rates are at the time. Or explore selling your house and renting instead. Owning a home imposes costs far in excess of the mortgage payment since you have taxes, repairs and maintenance to pay for as well.

If selling and then renting isn't palatable, or if refinancing doesn't make sense financially, then examine the possibility of selling your current house and buying a less expensive home. How much can you realistically pocket by selling your house (include realtor commissions and other fees), and how much would you realistically have to spend (include closing costs) to buy a less expensive home that still meets the family's needs?

If the family has two cars, can you survive with just one? Can the breadwinner commute relatively easily during the week by taking public transit, and is that practical? Axing a car eliminates insurance, gasoline, repair, upkeep, parking costs, registration costs and whatever car payment exists. While getting rid of a car might add a commuting expense for subways or trains or whatnot, the cost savings can outweigh the transit expenses, leading to a net gain in your budget. Beware, however, of breaking an auto lease; that can be expensive. Check with the dealer first to find out what options you have.

Reexamine your insurance policies. Shop around for equal coverage at lower prices. Life insurance, in particular, has been growing increasingly less expensive in recent years, and you might just find a policy equal to what you have now—but at a cost that is a few hundred dollars cheaper. Either call around to agents and get quotes that are apples-to-apples comparisons, or ask a local insurance broker to do the shopping for you. At the same time, look at increasing the deductibles on homeowner's and auto policies. A higher deductible can reduce your annual premiums by a few hundred dollars. Yes, you're on the hook for a great portion of any claim you have to file, but how often are you filing claims? Don't let the idea of paying the first $1,000 instead of the first $250 dissuade you from a higher deductible. The cost savings over the years will more than make up that one-time, $750 added cost—assuming you ever file a major claim.

Step 3: What niceties can you live without?

Certainly, there are many line items in your budget that are expendable: the money you waste every day on what are effectively throwaway items you really don't need (think: lattes, magazines, snacks or even the shirt or music download you buy on a whim) but which you happen to want or crave at the moment. You can slice many of those from your budget.

But don't automatically cut everything that falls under the definition of discretionary. That will prove counterproductive over time and provide an unrealistic view of your finances going forward. If your family lives for the weeklong summer vacation at the lake house you've been visiting for years, eliminating it and assuming you can do without it will likely cause regrets and a heightened sense that you're living like a pauper.

At some point, you're likely to rebel and pursue what, to you and your family, seem like important expenses. And that can throw your finances into disarray since your budget isn't structured to afford this.

Wiser instead to keep certain, important discretionary expenses in your budget. In some ways this is a lot like dieting: It's not about living a suddenly ascetic life, cutting out everything you enjoy; it's about moderation and feeling content with what you do purchase. So, rather than axing discretionary costs completely, scale them back. In this case, maybe you can keep the vacation, but reduce the number of days, find a less-expensive lake house to rent, or eliminate certain vacation activities you are OK living without.

Of course, keeping some of these expenses may mean you have to go back to Step 2 so that you can figure out where and how to trim some fixed costs.

Assuming you can make all these numbers work—that is, assuming you can keep your fixed costs and what you determine are necessary discretionary expenses comfortably below your one-paycheck income—you will have a budget that allows you to live on one income instead of two. Now, you can start preparing to pursue that path toward a one-income family.

What if the numbers don't seem to work, though?

Don't assume that forsaking that second paycheck is a doomed strategy. All is not necessarily lost.

IT'S NOT ALL ABOUT COSTS: CREATING ADDITIONAL INCOME

The true measure of success isn't defined by what you accomplish, but, rather, what you overcome.

In every endeavor, you almost always come upon an obstacle that would seem to mark the end of your expected path. And in terms of structuring a one-income lifestyle, the greatest financial obstacle is, unquestionably, the impression that you can't get there from here—that you can't make those bottom-line numbers work with your top-line income.

You might not be able to reduce your costs enough to ensure that a single income will support the family. And that might just be true . . . but it's true from a single vantage point: your costs. There's another factor in this equation: the income.

Do ways exist to increase the family's income?

Of course they do. You just have to think creatively.

A few pages back I said that the partner who wants to stay at home should spend time considering actionable solutions to address a spouse's worries about financial security. This is how you begin to think about those solutions:

First, you and your spouse need to define your combined goals. What do you want to accomplish? Are you trying to create an environment where a parent is home every day to take the kids to school, pick them up, ferry them to and from extracurricular activities, and then make sure they do their homework? Do you want to be at home only to raise an infant in the years before school starts? Are you looking for a reason to escape a job or career you don't like? Do you want to return to school to pursue a different vocation?

Whatever the case, an honest assessment of the answer to that question—What are your goals?—begins the conversation about how to develop alternative ways of making the budget work. If you each know what defines the finish line, you can map the course to get there.

So, for instance, you want to stay at home with an infant child. Well, it's clear a part-time job away from the house won't accomplish your goal. However, a part-time job *in your house* could. Think about it: Infants take naps. Can you use those hours to create home-based income? Depending on your career, you might provide consulting work to your current employer or other employers in that field. What opportunities might you have to freelance? In an Internet age, technology makes a wide variety of possibilities, well, possible.

If your career doesn't offer consulting or freelance prospects, spend some time researching home-based business opportunities online. They're all over the place. Not all are legitimate, and many either make no sense or will end up costing you more than you earn. You certainly don't want that. Then again, many can be as profitable as you need them to be. I have a family friend who left a lucrative career as an attorney to devote her days to her young children. She found a legitimate, natural-cosmetics company that allowed her to work from home, around her kids' schedules. Ultimately, she replaced almost the entirety of her former paycheck.

Or maybe you don't want to forsake your career but you do want to create a more balanced life in which your children don't have to miss out on crucial quality time with Mom and Dad by spending their before- and after-school hours in a daycare facility, or by coming home to an empty house or to one inhabited by a babysitter. Well, what if instead of leaving your job completely, you restructure your hours around a part-time schedule that allows you to come in after dropping your kids off at school and leave in time to retrieve them in the afternoon? Making this work can take many forms, including altering your career track to take a less demanding job with your employer, or changing your job duties to reduce your workload. Maybe you change job titles but stay in a related field; for example, a health care professional might return to her former duties as a floor nurse and only work particular hours or particular days.

Keep in mind, however, that part-time employment can be just as taxing as full-time work and can lead to even greater levels of personal frustration and stress. You may have to accept a job well beneath your qualifications that you ultimately find mind-numbing. Conversely, if you remain with the same employer, bosses accustomed to your work might expect a similar volume of production from you, despite new, limited hours.

Another solution: Both of you restructure your work hours. In some families I know, one parent gets the kids ready each morning and takes them to school while the other parent heads to work early. The parent who managed the kids' morning works later into the afternoon or evening while the early-work parent takes the afternoon shift with the kids, picking them up from school, managing the homework and transporting them to various extracurricular activities. With such a strategy, you effectively create stay-at-home parenting, while also creating cost savings by eliminating child-care expenses.

The message here is that while addressing the cost side of your budget is certainly necessary, overlooking the income side is shortsighted. The two work in tandem to help you live the life you ultimately want. Success just requires some creativity. And that creativity is where the real communication begins, because the best ideas you'll come up with as a couple will come from brainstorming various possibilities together. Don't feel pressure to find the solutions on your own. Talk with each other.

No two brains think alike. The idea you think is great might be untenable for reasons you don't see. Or the idea you think is goofy might just spark in your partner a slightly tweaked version that is perfect for the situation. When you're bouncing ideas off each other, you force the consideration of all the good, bad and ugly possibilities that might arise. It's in that give-and-take that the most creative solutions emerge. It is also where you two will find the common ground that you're both comfortable pursuing.

Most important, you will be working as a team—the goal of any healthy marriage.

PREPARATION IS THE SMARTER PART OF VALOR

To borrow a line from the Boy Scouts, "Be prepared."

Family finances can be fragile. An unexpected illness, a wrecked car, a job loss—these situations can destroy the best-laid financial plans. The costs of dealing with any of these crises can be enough to send your family into an economic tailspin if you're ill-prepared to handle them.

As such, before you do choose to move to one income, build your defenses first. In this case, that means building an emergency savings account.

Once you determine that it is financially feasible to live on one paycheck, don't rush to put your plan in place. Both of you should continue to work, but begin structuring your finances around that single income, to the degree that you can. Put your cost-savings plan into action and funnel into a bank account as much of the savings as you can to fatten your emergency account.

How much you need depends on your level of comfort and how much money the remaining breadwinner brings home each month.

Go back to your budget and look again at how much you must pay each month in fixed costs. These are the only costs that really matter. In a financial emergency, you're not going to be taking vacations and eating dinner out. You're going to be husbanding your available cash as you manage the emergency. Ultimately, you want some multiple of your monthly fixed expenses. This is where your comfort level comes in.

Common wisdom says you should have at all times between three and six months' worth of after-tax income stashed away in an account that you touch only—*only*—in a true emergency. So, if you bring home, say, $4,000 a month, you theoretically need $12,000 to $24,000 set aside. But you have to ask yourselves if you're both comfortable with either amount. One of you might be; the other, possibly not. (After-tax income is clearly more than your fixed costs—hopefully—so four to six months of after-tax cash could actually cover the family's spending needs for many more months.)

In this particular debate, the best solution is to err on the side of prudence. The bigger the account, the better the family's financial situation. But that doesn't mean if one of you feels fine with two months and the other says two years that you save up two years' worth of cash. This should be a negotiated bargain. Find the lowest common denominator you both can live with. Maybe it's ten months. Whatever the number, try as best you can to base the discussions on realistic assumptions. If your biggest concern is the loss of a job, don't base your comfort zone on the assumption that the working spouse will find a job quickly or, conversely, will be out of work forever.

What are the skills that spouse uses in the job now, and what's the demand in that industry? If the breadwinner is a nurse, job loss is likely to be temporary at worst, given demand in health care and the variety of work options. In that comfort zone of two months to two years, you might realistically opt as a couple for a spot somewhere along the shorter end of the spectrum. If the working spouse is employed by the last maker of typewriter ribbons, and the skills don't translate easily across industries, then moving toward the high end of that spectrum makes a lot more sense.

Just remember, each of you needs to feel comfortable that the family will be able to avoid financial ruin in the case of an emergency while still enjoying life to some degree. Otherwise, moving toward a one-income household is going to create anxiety and arguments.

HOME-EQUITY LINE OF CREDIT: THE EMERGENCY LIFELINE

In keeping with the theme of "Be prepared," open a home-equity line of credit at your local bank or credit union before one of you stops working. This is your fail-safe. (This assumes, of course, that you own a home; if not, you can skip this sidebar.)

In the event that your emergency savings proves insufficient in a financial emergency, the line of credit provides access to funds to pay your expenses until the emergency passes. As you would with your emergency savings account, only tap into this credit to pay your basic, fixed costs. Accumulating interest-bearing expenses for movies, restaurant meals and other clearly discretionary expenses is foolhardy even in normal times, and it is particularly so in a financial crisis.

The reason you want to have this line of credit in place before one of you leaves the workforce is that two incomes always look better than one when bankers are assessing your worthiness as a potential borrower. For that matter, you certainly don't want to wait until an emergency is upon you before you go searching for a line of credit. One of the perverse realities of banking is that banks are more than eager to accommodate your needs when you have no need to borrow, and are less than eager when your wallet is at its neediest. Banks rightfully worry about your ability to repay. By seeking a home-equity line before you need it, and when your finances look their best, you greatly increase your odds of a banker agreeing to offer you the line of credit.

Just remember, once you tap into your credit line, you are accumulating interest every month on the sum you've withdrawn, meaning you are actually increasing your monthly financial obligations since you will have to repay the borrowed sum every month. So be judicious about pulling money from a credit line.

The choice between one income or two is one of the most potentially problematic issues couples face during pregnancy. Ultimately, this chapter is about seeking answers through communication. Couples who are incapable of talking about money, however, will have trouble managing the demands of this discussion.

Purposefully forsaking an income is not an easy decision to make, particularly in an economy where two incomes often seem so necessary. Nor is this decision one you should make hastily or without a well-designed game plan. You must know how a single income will stretch across the family's financial needs and how you can trim costs to fit your lifestyle into a shrunken income stream. Only then can you properly prepare your finances to help you not only meet your financial aims but protect your family against potential hardships.

All that said, a happy, prosperous family life can be lived on one income. Couples opt for this lifestyle all the time. Indeed, during the six yeas I wrote the nationally syndicated "Love & Money" column for *The Wall Street Journal* Sunday supplement, readers routinely sent me e-mails describing how they came to the decision to give up one of their two incomes, the challenges they faced and met and the budgets they had to rework. And I can't think of one example where the writer didn't express heartfelt happiness at having made this decision.

So just because you can't see how to get there from here, it doesn't mean getting there is not possible. It just means you and your partner have some work to do first.

2

. . . .

Earning

MAKING MONEY IS THE FOUNDATION
OF EVERY FINANCIAL LIFE

To kids, money seems to be an unlimited resource. And why shouldn't they think that?

Regardless of whether your family is wealthy or not so wealthy, just about all of us are out buying everything from groceries to cars to clothes to burgers on the way home from the mall. All of us routinely interact with the economy in some fashion, and our kids see it all. They see us handing green paper to the cashier, writing checks, punching in secret codes for the debit machine or swiping our credit cards at the gas station. They see us stopping by the ATM to replenish our wallet. But these observations lack the context necessary to understand all those purchases.

In short, kids rarely see the physical effort that went into earning the money we spend, or the mental gymnastics we sometimes struggle with when it comes to spending. All they know is that if you want something, you basically just go get it.

But money, as we parents know far too well, is a far too limited resource. What you earn takes effort, and that effort means you exercise some degree of caution when it comes to spending. You spend on what you have to, and you apportion whatever remains to a few affordable discretionary purchases. This, then, is the first financial lesson kids need to learn from Mom and Dad:

> **Kids & Money Rule #1:** Spending money happens only after you earn it.

Teaching the concept of "earning," though, is the challenge. Kids aren't generally employed. So how do you teach earning when they don't earn?

That's where allowances come in.

Allowances: My First Payday

The most important fact about allowances is that your child earns one—though some parents might disagree with that statement. So let me explain.

Some parents subscribe to the idea that whatever their kids need, Mom and Dad will provide. If Mom and Dad don't provide it, then the kids didn't need it to begin with. Thus no need for an allowance exists. That's certainly an option, and it's fine up to a point. But it really doesn't teach children about the earning, spending and savings decisions they will need to make throughout their adult life.

At some point, kids become independent creatures, meaning they don't think precisely as you do and they place a different value on items than you do. For example, you might think that spending $29.95 on yet another video game is entirely too wasteful. Kids, in their own cost-benefit analysis, might think it's a fantastic use of financial resources: I spend $29.95 for a game that's going to keep me entertained for hundreds of hours over multiple days and months, and I can share this fun with my friends at school and in the neighborhood. That's, like, pennies a day for my enjoyment, and that's easily worth the price.

You don't have to agree with that analysis, but there is a certain kid logic to it. And while you absolutely have the obligation to share your values with your kids, to explain why you harbor them, and to try to instill some of the most important ones, you cannot impose your financial values on your children by fiat. Kids must learn to make their own financial decisions, if only to make the mistakes that will underscore your underlying beliefs. Your child deciding to spend $29.95 on a video game you think is wasteful is one of those decisions. If you let your kids learn these lessons through their own spending, you can be pretty sure that some of your values will be reflected in their actions as they mature.

That's why an allowance can be so important. It provides the funds necessary for shifting the responsibility of a decision onto your child's shoulders. It should be relatively easy to implement as well because kids want their own money to make their own decisions—particularly in those moments when Mom and Dad say "no" simply because Mom and Dad don't want to spend the money, don't have the money to spend or think the item in question is frivolous. With their own cash, kids have some economic freedom to buy what they want. (Note: I'm not implying that every child should have free rein to buy what he or she pleases, regardless of what Mom and Dad say. Any item that violates the family's set of core beliefs is off-limits, regardless of who has the money or what the item costs. Parents remain the final arbiter in all such decisions.)

Aside from infrequent gifts of cash received for birthdays and holidays, an allowance is often the only money kids can rightly call their own. As such, money carries an emotional component, just as it does for parents. Kids like the feeling of self-sufficiency just as much as we do, even if their version of "sufficient" is just $20 in a sock drawer.

If you refuse to pay an allowance, you will always face the cries of "I want" without being able to say, "You have your own money. If you really think this is how you want to spend it, then go ahead." Worse, you end up sending messages that are potentially contradictory. Why did you say no to this $29.95 video game, but yes to another similarly priced purchase on a different day? Why did one sibling get to buy something when, on another occasion, the other sibling didn't? You might have perfectly defensible reasons for each action, but kids aren't mentally equipped to process all of that; they just know that something seems unfair.

Allowances are one of the single best tools parents have when it comes to teaching kids about money. Everything that kids ultimately need to know about dollars and cents—saving, spending, investing, donating—is wrapped up in the humble allowance. Nevertheless, a survey by Yankelovich Partners shows that 40% of kids don't get one. This is a problem because, if kids don't earn an allowance, it is exceedingly hard for them to learn about the mechanics of daily finance. And that's a significant problem in America. A Federal Reserve survey from 2006 found that high school seniors answered correctly only about half the questions on personal finance and economics. That's not good, and you could argue a strong case that America's financial ineptness was part of the cause of the housing bubble and credit crisis that swept across the country in 2007 and 2008. Consumers had spent more than a decade putting much of their life on credit cards, spending just about every penny they earned and mistakenly using their artificially valued houses as ATMs to extract money for discretionary purchases—all the while largely ignorant about the side effects of their actions. When the house of cards crumbled, personal financial lives were upended or destroyed.

As parents, it's our job to make sure our kids understand money so that they don't suffer the same fate. Paying them an allowance is the first step.

There is no one correct approach to allowances. Parents all over the world have their own distinct views of when to pay, how much to pay and whether the payment should be tied to chores or schoolwork—or even whether it should be revoked as punishment for misdeeds. Ultimately, the decisions you and your spouse make will be based on your family's values. But as long as you begin to pay an allowance, and use that allowance to teach the lessons of money, you're on the right path.

WHEN TO BEGIN PAYING AN ALLOWANCE

As soon as your child expresses an interest in what money can buy, you should begin thinking about paying an allowance.

That's not to say the minute your two-year-old points to the candy display near the supermarket checkout line and wants a chocolate bar that you should rush home and start formulating your allowance scheme. The spending desires I'm talking about are for discretionary, consumer purchases such as toys, collectible playing cards and such. And that leads to another rule:

....
: **Kids & Money Rule #2:** When kids start asking parents to drive :
: to Toys "R" Us to buy some plastic whatnot, the time has come :
: to start thinking about an allowance. :
....

Typically, this is going to happen at about four or five years old. That doesn't mean you have to start paying an allowance at that age, though. And it doesn't mean the allowance you do pay has to be money. An early allowance scheme—one designed to acclimate kids to the concept of earning something of value that can then be spent on something of similar value—can begin with a system based on points or stickers. On a chart stuck to the refrigerator, you award points or stickers for tasks that you clearly assign. As those tasks are completed in the course of a day or over a week, you award the appropriate number of points/stickers. In turn, a predetermined number of points/stickers can be exchanged for something your child values highly, like a special dinner with Mom and Dad at your child's favorite restaurant, or a movie, computer time, extended TV or video game time or a trip to the toy store to pick out a toy that costs no more than some preset amount.

Offer a range of options over a range of point totals, making some of the lesser-valued awards reachable with a few days' or even a single day's effort. More valuable items should take a week or two, or longer, so that your child learns to delay gratification and save for something bigger or more important.

You'll know when the time has come to move from points and stickers to real dollars and cents. Kids are generally ready for a real allowance once they can:

- easily count, as well as add and subtract;
- differentiate between the different bills and coins;
- demonstrate an obvious interest in money;
- and clearly exhibit a desire for discretionary purchases that you don't always want to fund.

A child who is, say, struggling with numbers or has no obvious interest in money probably isn't ready to deal with an allowance. So wait. And don't worry that you're missing your opportunity. You're not. Just stick to the points/stickers system for a little longer. As kids grow, they will reach a point where their interest in money and an allowance becomes blindingly clear. Until that time, don't fret.

HOW MUCH TO PAY

This answer ranges all over the place, because how much you pay is a function of your income, what part of the country you're in and even the social setting in which your kids interact. A low-income child who attends public school in, say, New Mexico is going to earn an entirely different allowance than a child from a wealthy family who attends private school in, say, Boston. Those kids run in different socioeconomic brackets, face a different set of cost expectations among their peers and live in areas of the country where costs are wildly divergent. Out of necessity, their allowances are going to be different.

Even within the same neighborhood, though, disparities often exist. Parents all place a different value on what amount is appropriate for their kids. Some parents start by paying their kids 25 cents a week. Others pay a sum equal to the child's age so that a five-year-old earns $5; some cut that arithmetic in half. There is no one correct answer. You have to determine what feels right for your family based on the norms in your area and your family's set of values.

Whatever the case, the goal of an allowance is to teach kids money-management skills. Therefore, the next rule:

Kids & Money Rule #3: The size of an allowance should not be so meager that your child is a pauper among peers, nor so generous that your child can easily afford all wants with little financial planning.

Those pauper kids might just grow up to hoard money because they never feel like they're going to have enough, while those overpaid kids might grow up unprepared to plan their finances because they've always had more than enough to buy everything they want. Neither is a healthy money mentality.

Don't worry too much, initially, about the size of the allowance. Pick a number that feels right for your child based on whatever method feels most comfortable to your family. When kids first earn an allowance, the number is basically meaningless; they are just happy they have their own money. Soon enough you'll know if you're over- or underpaying. If your child is constantly buying things and never asking you to top-up the account to afford something, there's a good chance you're much too generous. You can cut the size of the payout or just skip the raises for a year or two. If they never seem to be able to afford anything they want with their own money, or complain about how other kids get a bigger allowance, chances are you're paying too little. Ask how much three or four of their closest friends earn and pay the average of those sums.

WHEN TO PAY

Most allowances are paid weekly. That's been standard operating procedure for generations. And it works fine, particularly with younger children who need the consistency of a regular payday or otherwise lose interest. Ultimately, it's fine to continue the weekly scheme until your child no longer needs your financial support.

But there is a savvier approach.

Again, because an allowance is a teaching tool and not just a distribution of cash, you need to use it to teach the lessons you want your kids to learn. And some of the lessons an allowance can teach come by altering the period between paydays. This is particularly useful as kids age and their spending demands and needs change.

For instance, when your kids are 11 or 12, you might consider paying the allowance monthly instead of weekly. Doing so effectively forces your youngster to begin thinking about how to stretch the cash across the entire month. At first, four weeks' worth of allowance is going to make a kid feel rich. Some kids might even blow the bulk of the payout immediately. But that's fine; it's a lesson learned. Having to spend the rest of the month without access to money means that mistake probably won't be made again. (Note: Paying monthly instead of weekly actually reduces your child's income. Monthly pay means that instead of 52 weekly allowances, you are actually paying just 48 weeks each year—12 months times 4 weeks per month. To remedy that, calculate a year's worth of weekly allowance and divide by 12 to determine the accurate monthly amount.)

When your kids hit eleventh or twelfth grade, consider paying the allowance for an entire semester. Open a checking account at a local bank for your son or daughter (more on that in an upcoming chapter) and deposit a semester's worth of money all at once. Tell your kids that this is all the cash you'll be dishing out until next semester, and that if they run out, tough luck.

While you're at it, deposit a separate amount that you would have otherwise spent on new school clothes. A parent can go broke living up to the sartorial whims of a teenager in high school. So don't try. Buy a few basic items that you'd normally buy, then deposit a sum in your child's checking account to pay for the trendy wear that kids all insist they need. Make abundantly clear that this sum represents all the money you're willing to spend on clothing. Tell your child if he spends recklessly on one shirt, one pair of pants and a single pair of new shoes, then he's going to look fairly foolish wearing the same outfit day after day.

You'll be surprised at just how unimportant certain fashion wants become when kids are charged with having to spend their own money.

This is also the time when kids start landing first jobs and will begin earning their own paycheck (and we'll cover kids and jobs in a later chapter). You can handle this period in a few ways. You can factor into your allowance calculations how much your child earns and reduce the allowance by a similar amount, or you can continue paying the same amount, since it is supposed to largely fund school and clothing needs, and let your child use their own earned income to pay for the discretionary purchases of youth—the movies, concerts, gas money, etc. Or if you want to encourage your child to work—particularly a child who seems not to appreciate the value of a dollar and the effort needed to earn it—you can scale back the allowance by some amount and tell your child that she is of an age now where she can make up the difference with her own labor.

Once your kids are in college, pay six months' or the entire year's worth of allowance—as well as whatever educational and housing costs you're footing—at the start of each semester or school year. Now, you're forcing kids to plan long-term and to manage their finances with an eye toward affording not only the one-off, big-ticket costs of their college fees, but also their housing or living costs each month, as well as their entertainment and clothing expenses.

Again, clearly state that this is all the money you're putting up for the semester or year, and that if the money runs out, then your child will have to find a way to earn the necessary income. As an incentive to save, offer this inducement: "Whatever you have remaining in your account at the end of the school year, I will double it and put it in a savings account for you to have after graduation."

By altering the way you pay, you teach your kids to grow increasingly smarter about how they manage money and increasingly confident in their ability to plan their spending and saving for longer than a week. Those are lessons that will serve them well when they're adults faced with the sundry ways of destroying their financial security through misguided decisions about money. At this age, you could take allowance a step further and allow your kids to negotiate how much discretionary spending money you add over and above the funds necessary to college costs. Financial negotiation is clearly a part of adult life, from negotiating salaries to rents to new car purchases, and this can be an opportunity to help a child learn that skill. Have your college student present a compelling, reasoned argument for why a larger allowance is needed. Grade the argument on its merits and make your decision. If the answer is "no," explain where the argument failed and offer your child a second—maybe even third—chance to make the case.

WHAT ACTIVITIES EARN AN ALLOWANCE

By and large, an allowance should be given with few strings attached. This is a tool to teach money-management skills. You're not trying to teach your kids how to be employed; that will come when they're old enough to start babysitting or mowing lawns or seeking other forms of youth-appropriate jobs.

As such, this might more accurately be titled, "What *not* to pay for."

Too often too many parents tie their kids' allowance schemes to chores or routine schoolwork. Neither is a good idea. You're paying for what should be completed without financial incentive. Thus, our next rule:

> **Kids & Money Rule #4:** Good grades are expected, and helping around the house is simply the price of family life.

Parents who establish in their children the unrealistic financial expectation that kids deserve to be paid for everything they do in life don't serve their kids well. Money is rarely handed out in everyday life simply for doing what's right or what is expected, so there's no reason to ingrain that expectation early on.

But there's a more practical reason to avoid paying for school-work or chores: When kids reach the point where they feel they have enough money for the time being, they no longer have an incentive to meet your demands. And all too often they don't, particularly when they're older and earning outside income from a part-time job. In that case, you're lost and you have little leverage. More often than not, you end up doing the chore yourself, undermining the parent/child relationship because you've put the power to say "no" in your child's hands—all because your child didn't want or need money at that moment.

When kids ask for pay tied to their basic, required chores—and I promise they will ask this at some point—you can respond by saying, "Okay. But just so we're all on the same page, if I'm going to start paying you to clean your room and take out the garbage, then you're going to start paying me for cooking your meals and cleaning your clothes. And the way I calculate it, you're going to owe me a lot more than I'm willing to pay you for your chores. But we can try it your way, if you really want to." Ultimately, kids have to learn the value of contributing to their family's upkeep.

All that said, kids should be able to earn money for chores that go beyond their normal duties. You want to encourage industriousness and a work ethic and provide a way for your children to earn that extra income they seek. So, if your daughter's unpaid obligation is to make her bed every morning, then maybe she can earn extra money by making Mom and Dad's bed, too. If one of your son's unpaid chores is to clean his room every Saturday before going out to play, maybe he can earn extra cash by vacuuming the house or cleaning the bathrooms. Whatever the case, make the unpaid and paid chores age-appropriate. At age five, my son came outside one late fall day to ask me if he could rake the yard to earn the $3 he wanted to buy a pack of the trading cards he collected at the time. Raking leaves was not on his list of expected chores, and I was pleased that he saw me doing the work and figured he could earn additional money by taking over the duty for me.

At his age, though, he had no hope of raking our yard, and it would have been unfair to pay him only $3 if he had done so. But his gumption was well-placed and appreciated. So I gave him a small, $3 patch of yard to complete for me, including raking and bagging. It was a chore appropriate to his age and abilities. You don't want to give your kids work that's beyond their means, or you will set them up for failure and disappointment. Better all around to assign tasks at which they will succeed so that completing the job and earning the money creates a sense of accomplishment, which will naturally instill the notion that work isn't so bad after all.

WHAT THE ALLOWANCE SHOULD COVER . . . OR NOT

First off, the allowance should never be so big that it can cover the routine expenses of raising a child—basic shoes and clothing, food, educational costs and such. These are not expenses that should be borne by a child—though, as I pointed out a few pages back, they can be incorporated into an allowance scheme for older high school and college-age children when you want to pay them a lump sum to manage a larger portion of their costs. That said, parents should not slough off their obligations onto their children.

Instead, an allowance should cover those extraneous consumer purchases kids seek out on their own after talking with friends or watching TV commercials. This might include the trendy clothes for school, a new video game or game system, a spur-of-the-moment desire to buy a toy while out shopping with parents, or souvenirs while on vacation that go beyond a specified value that Mom and Dad are willing to pay. If your child has the money on hand, you don't pay. If your child has conveniently forgotten the cash at home, you have two choices:

- pay, but demand immediate repayment the moment you get home. Kids are quite adept at buying on credit and then conveniently forgetting they owe Mom or Dad some cash.
- refuse to pay, and remind your child of the need to carry cash when headed to a shopping center. If you have the time and inclination, you can offer to return to the store later that day or the next day, or some other convenient time over the next week so that your child can make this purchase. If that item is that important, kids will agree, albeit reluctantly and with great moodiness at times, or they will ultimately forget or decide it's not that important after all.

There should be certain items that remain on the Do Not Buy list, regardless of whose money is involved. If you wouldn't buy your son a BB gun because you oppose firearms, then clearly that's one of your family's core values, and allowance money can't be used to undermine these values.

ALLOWANCES AND PUNISHMENT

At some point, every parent threatens to revoke all or part of an allowance for some misdeed. You do it because it can be so effective. An allowance is generally a kid's only source of cash, and the threat of losing it is powerful motivation to shape up.

But again, this isn't such a wise idea.

With this strategy, you're tying money to power. A parent is in a superior role when applying punishment for misdeeds, and money shouldn't be wrapped up in that conversation. You create the impression that money is an incentive for being good, and that's never the case. Money is earned, money is spent, but it is never awarded for simply following the conventions of society or, more specifically, your family. As such, it should not be granted or revoked based on a child's behavior.

The threat of losing an allowance can be a powerful motivation for kids to put money above all else, including the truth. Clearly, that's not a healthy relationship to have with your finances as an adult, so it shouldn't be a relationship you encourage through the punitive measures you impose on your child for transgressions. Learn, instead, from my mistake. My wife and I tried to use money as punishment when our son was about six years old. He had just started receiving his allowance, and he knew that misbehaving in school or disobeying Mom and Dad meant that he could lose his money for the week. He understood—all too well.

For a while, all was fine . . . and then it happened. He came home from school one afternoon and surreptitiously slipped something into the trash behind his back.

His mom noticed the not-so-smooth maneuver. When he walked away, she reached into the garbage can and fished out what was a letter from his teacher announcing that our son had acted up in class and had not listened when he was told to stop horsing around with a friend.

Confronted with the evidence, he broke down in tears and

said he'd tried to hide it because he didn't want to lose his only dollar for the week.

He did, in fact, lose it—not for acting up in class, but for his dishonesty. Afterward, my wife and I scolded ourselves for putting our son in a position where money was so important. We quickly revised the rules of the house and did away with any punishments related to money. The result: He has always owned up to misdeeds and he began to save his money instead of rushing to spend it. In fact, money, though clearly relevant to his life, never really took center stage with him again.

It comes down to this: Money is never a good disciplinary tool with children. Kids do not learn to manage money so much as they learn to manage Mom and Dad's expectations for fear of losing their only source of capital. That has no long-term benefits.

Instead, pay the allowance as agreed upon, even if your kid has misbehaved, but revoke other privileges instead, like access to the TV, the computer, the phone, a favorite video game or toy. With older children, say no to movies with a friend or a school party, or take away access to the car or computer or, particularly, a cell phone (teens go nuts without the ability to access their social circle through text messaging and mobile phone communications).

WHEN TO CHANGE YOUR ALLOWANCE SCHEME

Every once in a while, you might need to revisit the allowance you pay. Kids change, situations change, and the way you pay an allowance might need to change, too.

I'm not just talking about increasing the payout at some regular interval—though you do need to do that to keep pace with kids' increased spending needs as they age. No, I'm talking about a wholesale revision of your kid's allowance scheme.

This could happen for any number of reasons, but it always comes back to the fact that something's not working right, and you clearly recognize that. An example from my life: My wife and I had been paying our son his standard weekly allowance for about five years when we began to notice that items he wanted to purchase were often pricier than his wallet could afford. As a result, he was routinely hitting us up for a loan to cover his shortfall. The problem was that his weekly pay wasn't big enough to cover the cost of some items, and he didn't have the patience to save for them. What he wanted was a much bigger payday that would allow him to afford those bigger costs.

My wife and I saw this as a perfect opportunity to begin encouraging him to think about stretching his money and budgeting. We surmised—correctly, it turned out—that he would learn necessary lessons early on by spending all of his money quickly and then suffering until his next payday. So we changed his allowance to pay him his entire allowance monthly. That would give him a larger wad of cash that, after saving his mandatory amount, he could spend however he wished. But, we told him, the minute it's all gone, it's all gone, "Don't come to us two weeks from now complaining you have no more money for the rest of the month." He was fine with that, and—after initially spending too much at once—did a pretty good job of spending on big items every once in a while, spending nothing some months, and generally not whining when he ran out of cash early in the month.

None of this is to imply that you can't adjust an allowance downward, if needed. If in a rotten economy Mom or Dad lose a job, or must take a new job that pays less, kids might have to accept a smaller outlay as well. Use such episodes as teachable moments that serve to show kids how financial setbacks require families to alter their budget and their lifestyle to fit their new financial reality.

Often parents find that talking to their children about these kinds of setbacks is challenging, and feel they shouldn't foist such heavy adult problems onto a child's shoulders. That's understandable. But kids are savvier than parents want to believe, and more resilient. They sense when financial struggles have beset their family, and they are typically willing to sacrifice their lifestyle, too, to help their parents. So be open and frank with them about the situation the family is confronting. Be honest, but certainly you don't want to freak them out with dire projections. To the degree you can, assure them that the family will survive this rough period. If you've built a financial cushion through the years that you will rely on to help support the family during this time, highlight that effort as an example of the financial preparation adults must plan into their budget in good times so that when sour times arise there's a buffer to deflect the full force of the blow.

Whether up or down, don't be afraid to tweak an allowance scheme when it clearly needs tweaking. You can use those moments to better tailor the financial lessons you want to teach.

WHEN TO STOP PAYING AN ALLOWANCE

In general, stop paying an allowance when your child no longer needs your financial assistance. In many instances that's when a student graduates college and joins the workforce. In other cases it could be sooner, when your high school–aged offspring generates sufficient income from their own work. As I'll discuss in the next section on kids and jobs, the Internet specifically,

and technology broadly, has given teens the ability to generate meaningful income on their own through online commerce
or technological services they might render, such as helping
others deal with computer problems or other such issues.

At 12 years old, my son—the typical preteen video game
junkie—hot-wired one of his game controllers to perform
a specific function the controller wasn't built to perform but
which gave him an advantage in the online shoot-'em-up games
he enjoys. He decided that with a little effort, he could modify
controllers for other people and sell them online for $75 to
$100 a pop, representing a fat profit margin, and, with the sale
of a single controller, more money than he'd get from a month's
worth of allowance.

Such opportunities are widespread, and if your child taps
into one it might be the case that he's earning substantially more
from his own efforts than he would from the allowance. In that
case, eliminating the allowance might make sense. If you choose
that route, explain why you're doing so. You might also offer to
redirect the allowance money into another use beneficial to your
child. That might mean adding the sum to a college fund, or,
assuming your child's income is reportable on tax returns to the
Internal Revenue Service, you might offer to use the allowance
money to fund an Individual Retirement Account (an IRA) that
over the decades will grow into a sum that can help your child
retire more comfortably (more on this later in this chapter).

Finally, you might want to cut the allowance cord if your
college graduate moves back home without a job and starts to
live off Mom and Dad's efforts once again. To some degree, you
might tolerate a few months of this as your young adult searches
for work. But if the job search effort seems lackluster, or if con-
tinuing to pay an allowance is counterproductive, cutting off

the cash flow quickly becomes an incentive to find meaningful employment.

Help Wanted: Kids and Jobs

I grew up having to earn my spending money. My grandmother and grandfather—who largely raised me—never had a lot of disposable income. While they would always slip me three or four dollars (the equivalent of less than $10 these days) when I went somewhere with friends, my extraneous consumer wants largely came from whatever income stream I could muster on my own. That started in about the seventh grade, when my friend Mike and I would push a lawnmower around the neighborhood, knocking on doors and soliciting our grass-cutting service for $10 a yard. In the fall, we raked leaves. When I could drive, we delivered phone books. In ninth grade I bagged groceries at a local supermarket. In tenth grade I flipped burgers. In twelfth I bused tables at a Tex-Mex eatery.

My point is that kids need to learn that money is a direct byproduct of the work they expend earning it. Only after kids actually sweat for their dollars can they appreciate the real value of spending them. When they're spending Mom and Dad's money (and I'm not talking about an allowance here) they'll gladly buy those $100 jeans at the fashionable, teen-centric boutique. The cost imparts no pain on their wallet. Yet when they're spending their own limited resources, particularly the money earned from their own work, they're more inclined to buy the $40 brand at the department store. In short, a stint of real-world employment helps make kids better stewards of the money that flows through their hands.

Of course, the challenge is getting kids to consider work these days. Look around: How often do you see kids doing the jobs we parents once did? You still see girls babysitting, but rarely do you see kids out cutting a yard or raking leaves. I occasionally see a teenager bagging groceries; sometimes they're busing tables. For the most part, though, professional lawn services or immigrant laborers handle yard work nowadays, and it's generally college kids or older workers in the service-oriented jobs that once were staples of employment for teens seeking spending money.

Several reasons exist for this. For one thing, affluence is far more widespread in America today than in previous generations, meaning kids don't necessarily have to work. And really, they don't have much incentive to work because they know they can easily tap into Mom and Dad's wallet for whatever spending money they want. That's because Mom and Dad struggle with a sense of guilt caused by spending so much time earning their own paycheck. Often, they try to make it up to their kids with material items or the cash necessary to buy them. Also, many parents nowadays don't want their younger children running around the neighborhood soliciting work out of fear of what might happen to them. Meanwhile, schoolwork and the extra-curricular activities needed to get into college have become so demanding that many kids and their parents would rather skip the part-time employment to manage all the other burdens.

All of that is understandable. Still, to be successful in their own lives later, kids must learn that money is the byproduct of labor—their *own* labor. And encouraging that labor . . . well, that's all up to you. There's certainly good reason why you might consider pushing your kids toward some form of appropriate work: A 2003 study by Roper ASW, a global marketing research and consulting firm, found that people who worked in high school are much more likely to achieve the financial goals they set, and grow up more knowledgeable about money and investing than those who didn't work when they were youngsters. And to allay worries that jobs eat into study time and, thus, tank a teen's grades, Temple University research found that kids working less than 10 hours a week in a job during the school year earned better grades than those who didn't work at all—though working in excess of 20 hours a weeks generally caused teens to "disengage from school," clearly not what you want.

WHEN SHOULD KIDS START WORKING?

Legally speaking, kids have to be 16 years old to work in non-agriculture-related jobs, and there are some exceptions that allow kids as young as 14 to seek employment. But let's stick with 16, since that's generally the age at which employers are willing to hire kids.

That doesn't mean kids have to wait that long. I was mowing lawns in seventh grade, which would put me at about 13 years old. And that's a fine age to start your kids thinking about the kinds of jobs they can handle, be it babysitting, yard work, car washes or even computer-oriented work and hobbies that might generate income.

Kids & Money Rule #5: While 16 is generally the legal age of employment, encourage kids starting around age 13 to think of ways they can earn an income.

That doesn't mean they absolutely *must* be earning their own spending money at 13 or 14 or so—only that this is a good age to start them in that direction. Only you know if your kids are really ready for that commitment. Do you see the necessary maturity? Are they capable of handling themselves professionally? Do you think they'll complete the task, or will they get tired or bored and leave the job partially completed? Do you see that they demonstrate a work ethic?

If they're not old enough to deal with the rigors of working, don't push work just yet. They will grow into it over time, and you will know when the right moment arises.

KID-FRIENDLY EMPLOYMENT

In previous generations, kids had a fairly limited selection of employment opportunities: babysitter, yard boy, fast-food restaurant employee, sales clerk in a mall boutique. And, clearly, those jobs still exist for kids, though, as I noted previously, you do often find college students—and even college graduates—increasingly snagging those jobs. But today's span of job possibilities is much larger because of the dramatic expansion of technology and the service industry.

As such, the job that might make the most sense for your child could be one that plays off a specialized interest your kid has. For instance, I know a kid who became so proficient at wakeboarding that he landed a job at a summer camp in his early teens teaching the sport to younger campers. The pay was good and he continued that job through college. Another was so talented on a skateboard that a local skate shop hired him to sell products and teach skateboarding to kids who wanted to know how to perform the various tricks. A third was so competent with stock-market research as a teen that he was paid by his father's small company to help research investments for the company's retirement plan (honestly; he was that good).

These aren't jobs that are necessarily advertised. They arise because a kid demonstrates an obvious proficiency with some particular skill or knowledge base and has the people skills necessary to convince a would-be employer of the wisdom of the hire.

Parents play a role in this. You need to help your children think creatively about employment opportunities that might fit their temperament and abilities. Your vegetarian daughter clearly isn't going to be flipping burgers at McDonald's the way you did as a teenager. Instead, encourage her to find a vegetarian restaurant in town or a natural-foods store where her interests better align with the employer's. Maybe your son is fluent in Spanish or Mandarin and can spend several afternoons a week teaching language classes to kids and adults. Maybe there are translation services he can offer to local businesses. Maybe there's an opportunity to offer translation services online. Indeed, don't overlook technology. Kids are tech junkies and news reports routinely feature youngsters who create retail-oriented websites or other technological offerings that find a ready, willing mass of consumers. Again, it speaks to building on the strengths and interests that a child harbors inside. As a parent, you'll know what those are because you undoubtedly see them.

Technology also offers job-search services online in communities all across the country. Sites like Snagajob.com have lots of listings for hourly work. Monster.com is an option as well. There's even CampJobs.com, which allows job seekers to post a résumé and search for job openings at summer camps around the United States and Canada. Teens with particular outdoor skills, like an Eagle Scout with expertise in orienteering, can find employment that matches their abilities and interests.

As a parent, you can also provide assistance by helping your child write a basic résumé and cover letter, clearly highlighting whatever special skills are appropriate. Help them role-play for the interviews they'll face. The effort you put into the exercise will be rewarded when you realize one day that your son or daughter is happy and financially independent.

Assuming your child isn't a wakeboarding star or linguist, here are a few areas where kids can find employment:

- **Babysitter or parental helper.** Don't knock babysitting. Kids are earning $10 to $15 an hour these days, a figure sharply higher than the federal minimum wage. And parents are willing to pay those prices. Parental helpers, meanwhile, are kids still a bit too young to take care of a child unattended, but they're earning $5 to $7 an hour looking after a child while a stay-at-home or even work-at-home parent completes certain tasks at home during the day.

- **House cleaning, car washing, lawn service.** These jobs are harder to come by since so many professional services now focus exclusively on these areas. Yet, if there are elderly relatives in your family who could use help keeping their house clean or their lawn tidy, that's a great place to start. Once your child has spent several weeks doing a nice job, ask the relative to spread the word among his or her peers. Other elderly people will be eager to find a dependable, trustworthy helper.

- **House- or pet-sitting or pet caretaker.** Know of anyone who travels frequently and who has a pet or house that needs tending to? Pet owners, in particular, are inclined to find someone who can come to their house to care for their animals, rather than take on the cost and sometimes emotional torment of sticking their beloved pooch or kitty in a kennel. Once you find one customer for whom you provide exemplary service, ask for referrals.

RETIREMENT SAVINGS

This is actually fodder for a later chapter, but I want to touch on it briefly here. Once your child has income that must be reported to the Internal Revenue Service (see sidebar below), start pushing a retirement-savings account such as a Roth IRA, even if that means you're the one who actually funds the account for your child.

WHEN IS CHILDHOOD INCOME REPORTABLE?

Technically, a child's income is reportable to the IRS if any *one* of the following four requirements is met:

- A child has unearned income from interest, dividends, capital gains, etc. that exceeds $900.
- A child has earned income (meaning from an employer) above $5,450.

- A child's gross income (meaning before taxes are paid) is greater than the larger of $900 or a child's earned income plus $300.
- Net earnings from self-employment exceed $400.

These requirements are as of the 2008 tax year, and they're likely to change over time, so consult a tax pro to determine whether your child has reportable income.

A Roth IRA grows tax-free and the withdrawals your child ultimately pulls out in retirement are tax-free as well. The Roth is the single best retirement account available, particularly for youngsters who will benefit from five decades of compounded growth. Just remember that to fund the account, your child needs to file a tax return that shows reportable income. But more on this in a bit.

For now, just get your child focused on earning money—not for the sake of the money, but for the life lessons a job will provide.

3

. . . .

Spending

YOU EARNED IT, SO ENJOY IT

The only purpose for earning money is—you guessed it—to spend it.

Now, don't read that in an overly consumerist way. Saving money is most assuredly one of the most crucial activities necessary for success in anyone's financial life. Still, think about it: What are you saving it for? To ultimately spend it, either relatively soon, when the next batch of bills comes in, or much later, when the nest egg you have accumulated throughout your career provides the paycheck you need for the spending you will do in retirement.

Living life obviously requires an outlay of cash for clothing, food, shelter, electricity and water, the most basic staples. Likewise, living life requires you spend money on the pursuit of some of life's niceties. As such, spending is a basic financial skill that kids must learn as they grow up. Because even before you can become a successful saver, you have to learn to be a wise spender—otherwise you'll have no money to save.

And what does "wise spender" mean in kid terms? Actually, the same thing it means for Mom and Dad:

- Understanding how a budget works and why adhering to one in some fashion is the cornerstone of learning to live within your means;
- Understanding the difference between *wants* and *needs* and how mistaking the two can destroy your budget; becoming a smart consumer by comparison shopping and buying only what you can afford;
- Understanding credit so that you'll never find your outflow exceeds your income.

And if the nation's consumer addiction is any indicator, the most important lesson is the hardest to teach: delayed gratification, or learning to put off for weeks, months, even years, the more expensive items that don't fit within the current confines of your budget.

The basic idea of spending—that is, handing over a portion of your money for some item—isn't very hard to teach. In fact, you don't even have to teach it, really. Kids naturally want to buy things; they get that from us parents. They see us spend money almost every day, and they learn through repetitive exposure just how the process works. About the only facet of this exchange that requires any hand-holding is a reminder early on to reclaim the change from the cashier when buying something. Younger kids often get so excited by the purchase that they'll eagerly hand over $10 for a $6 item and never think to care that they're due $4 in return. That recognition will come in time, but when you begin to allow your children to interact directly with the economy—to physically pay for their purchases—you're going to have to remind them to get their change and to count it to make sure the appropriate amount has been returned.

But let's start this chapter with delayed gratification, because learning to temper your wants—in other words, learning to spend prudently—is one of the most important building blocks in living within your means. From that flows everything else, such as the ability to budget and plan and save.

Delayed Gratification

Take a look at your own spending. What kind of message are you sending?

Do you see a slick, new mobile phone advertised on TV and buy it the next day? When you're out shopping and your child asks for a toy do you routinely say "Sure, Sweetie, we can buy that." Do you or your spouse openly covet what you don't have—a new car, a swimming pool in the backyard, diamond earrings—and then find a way to get it through a home-equity loan or credit card?

These are all very clear messages children cannot help but absorb and incorporate into their own financial lives. Don't think they're oblivious to this; they see it all, even when you think they're not paying attention. And the message is unambiguous: Whatever want arises can be sated, almost regardless of cost. That's the mentality that has so many American households—and America as a country—saddled by history's largest accumulation of debt, and it's a terrible mind-set to pass on to your kids.

Instead, parents need to send the message that, yes, consumer spending is okay, but only so long as it occurs within your financial means. That doesn't imply you live the life of a financial hermit. You can spend on the items that bring you happiness or enjoyment. But you can only do so to the degree that your wallet can afford that expense. If you can't make the purchase now, then the purchase must wait.

In other words, delayed gratification.

But this concept of putting off the purchase of something you want right now isn't the easiest for adults to learn or to teach. The challenge is only worse for kids, who have even less tolerance for waiting because their perception of time is so different. They effectively think in dog years. An hour is a day. A day is a week. And a week is pretty much "kill me now, because I'll be old and dead by then." Using words to describe delayed gratification, thus, is going to get you nowhere, really. They'll hear what you say, but it's not going to sink in well because "waiting" to buy a toy or a video game or some useless tchotchke from a grocery store vending machine isn't something kids are naturally equipped to do very well, particularly younger kids.

Instead, you can begin teaching the lesson early by using a game that will immediately make sense to them. It's a game one of my former colleagues used quite successfully with his two kids. It's called, "A Dollar or a Soda?"

Next time you're at a restaurant and your kids want to order a soft drink with their meal, offer this option instead: "You can have the soda, or you can have water and I'll give you the dollar your soda would have cost."

In other words: Satisfy your needs cheaply instead of immediately gratifying your wants, and you will have more money in your pocket.

Not every kid will take you up on the offer. Others, however, will end up drinking quite a lot of water and collecting quite a few dollars. Either way, the message is clear that as a consumer you have to evaluate the financial costs imposed by your wants. At first, you'll probably need to explicitly explain this lesson to your children, who might not immediately understand why you'd offer such a deal. You might have to offer that explanation more than once. Over time, however, your kids will come to recognize that the question you're trying to get them to think about is this: "Is feeding my want worth the price it will cost me?"

Wants vs. Needs: Which Is Which?

Listen to any child watching the Cartoon Network and you are bound to hear, "Mommy [or Daddy], I really need _____!" You can fill in the blank with anything from toys to games to a McDonald's Happy Meal that comes packaged with a new figurine tied to the latest animated movie. You will *never* hear a child say, "Mommy, I want new underwear!"

Kids almost always misinterpret wants and needs. Obvious reasons exist, not the least of which is the fact that younger kids, in particular, have no financial power of their own. Thus, to emphasize their desire for something, they categorize it as a "need" when it's clearly not. No kid *needs* a Happy Meal just for the toy—then again, no kid *wants* a Happy Meal solely for the food.

So it's up to us parents to demonstrate the difference.

One place to impart this message is in the supermarket aisles. Shopping for food is a task on every family's list. Lots of us shop without a plan, though. We pop into the market and stroll up and down the aisles, grabbing not just what the family needs, but a lot of what the family wants. These are often impulse purchases. "Oh, look . . . Rice Krispies Treats! Let's get a few boxes of those!" Likely you didn't go to the store thinking you needed Rice Krispies Treats, but you saw them, immediately wanted them, and, so, tossed the boxes into the basket without a second thought. Kids see that, and the message resonates: "I can buy what I want, too."

A better strategy: Make a grocery list, and make a game of it with your child.

Lists help focus the shopping exercise, limiting your purchases to what you deem most necessary, and, assuming you show some restraint, keeping you from grabbing every item that strikes your fancy. More important for this particular lesson, lists are a great way to help kids learn to differentiate between wants and needs. In most families, milk is a need. It's a product kids can immediately grasp as a need because otherwise they're eating dry cereal or dousing it with water or orange juice. Cookies are a want. They are a treat; treats are wants.

So start your grocery list with two columns—needs on one side, wants on the other—and together go through the pantry and refrigerator making note of items you might buy. As you do so, ask with each item: "Want or need?" Let your child answer, and then talk about it. Ask why your child thinks a particular item is a need or want. Praise the correct answer with a high-five or whatever other acknowledgment is common in your family, or correct his rationale if it's wrong and explain why it's incorrect. Then head to the store and shop together, following the list.

You want your kid with you at the store because there's a very good chance he's going to find something he wants that's not on the list. Again, this is a great opportunity to discuss whether the item is a need or want. If it's a want, don't immediately say no. Instead, talk about what your child or the family might give up on the "want" side of the grocery list in order to afford this new desire. Now, you're getting into the trade-offs that fiscally prudent people have to weigh every time competing wants arise. You certainly can't fund every want, so you have to choose. What is your child willing to sacrifice in order to buy this new want? Or, given that some other want must be sacrificed, is the new want really that important? Let him make that decision so that he feels the impact directly. He'll either be happy with his choice back at home, or he'll realize this was a bad trade and be wiser about his choices in the future. Of course, you might have to revisit the experience in the future, just as a mental nudge to remind him that "Last time you made a trade-off, you weren't happy with it, so are you sure you want to make this trade-off this time?"

A cardinal rule to remember:

Kids & Money Rule #6: Guide and advise your kids about money, but don't dictate.

Kids learn better when the lessons come from their own experiences, not when parents bark out rules. Similarly, kids fare far better when Mom and Dad offer praise for success and encouragement when failures happen. They don't do so well when parents criticize and belittle failures or times when kids don't choose what Mom or Dad would have chosen.

As kids age, put them in charge of their own list. In middle school, this can work with school supplies. Along with the mandatory needs like pencils and paper and notebooks, kids always have wants as a new school year approaches, such as a particular knapsack or locker accoutrements. In high school, it's clothes and shoes that go beyond the basic school attire you're willing to cover. In each case, give them a budget for their wants—a budget set in stone—and let them decide how to spread that limited cash across their often unlimited wants. Again, unless the items your kids want to buy violate family values, allow them to spend as they wish.

Pint-Sized Budgets

For many adults, "budget" is a four-letter word (albeit with two extra letters). Adults hate them. Budgets trigger a sense of confinement, forcing us to feel bad about spending our hard-earned cash on expenses that bring us joy.

In truth, budgets can be liberating. They show us where we're overspending; they give us insight into how we deploy our money; they allow us to better plan our future spending so that we don't fall into a cycle of debt that can haunt us our entire life. Budgets show us when we're spending on items that mean little or offer no real enjoyment, which, in turn, lets us instead shift that money into categories that provide greater happiness. (I'm not going to get into a big treatise here on budgeting, but, again, I would encourage you to read my first book in this series, *Financially Ever After: The Couples' Guide to Managing Money,* which details how to make easy-to-use budgeting strategies.)

Love them or not, budgets are a necessity and budgeting is a financial life skill. As such, kids need to learn how to build and live within the borders of their own pint-sized budget. Now that doesn't mean a six-year-old should be hunched over the kitchen table once a month figuring out how to stretch an allowance across packs of bubble gum, a new pair of shoes, and the unexpected cost of a laser tag party later in the month. Budgeting for kids is a much simpler affair, designed to show them that income has to be successfully distributed across competing needs, and that the income from one pay period needs to stretch across to the next. Otherwise you risk going without for possibly an extended period, or draining your savings you've worked so hard to accumulate for other, possibly more important, purposes.

Start the budgeting process at just about the same time you begin paying an allowance. The Three-Jar Budget is the conventional, tried-and-true strategy many parents use to first expose their kids to the idea that your limited amount of dollars have to serve multiple purposes. But a more practical approach, one that more closely mimics the way real life works, is to add a fourth jar to the equation.

THE FOUR-JAR BUDGET

Start with four jars. Yes, I know, pretty obvious. But they really don't have to be jars. Use whatever vessels work best—envelopes, bowls, four zippered pouches. Whatever.

The first three you label "Saving," "Spending," "Giving." That's the traditional trio. The fourth that we're adding to this is "Future Spending."

Saving: Into the Saving jar goes, wait for it, savings—the money that, once it reaches a preset amount, should be transferred to a kid-centric bank account.

Many local banks, particularly so-called community banks, savings and loans or credit unions, offer accounts geared toward kids, often with low or no account minimums. Some even send out monthly, kid-friendly financial education materials to help kids learn about banking and money. When kids hit about ten years old, consider an online savings account, which routinely sports markedly larger interest rates. And by the time your child is older, she will likely have a larger bank balance, meaning that with the online account she's not only building up a bigger balance in a quicker fashion, she'll more readily see the impact that earning interest can have on the account from one month to the next. With every statement, she could see several additional dollars, rather than a few cents, dumped into her account by the bank. (The next chapter, "Saving," more completely addresses how to build in your child a savings ethic.)

Giving: Into the Giving jar goes the share of money earmarked for charity or tithing. You can offer suggestions on how your child might donate this money, but provide several options. Too many parents get hung up on giving to the church during Sunday services, which is fine, but recognize that many other valuable opportunities exist that might better inspire your child to be munificent with money later in life, when giving matters most.

Look around town for charities and organizations that might resonate with a child—something like Special Olympics or a women's shelter that needs donations to buy new toys for the kids who live there. Maybe it's a local farm that takes in greyhounds after their racing career is over and the owners need donations to help care for the dogs.

Be careful, though, with forcing particularly young kids to give. They often don't understand why they have to give away a portion of their meager sum of money, regardless of what you tell them. Younger kids have a tough time comprehending the idea of "financial need," or the notion that others are less fortunate. Those are adult concepts, and kids have a far narrower field of vision. Unless they've experienced it personally, they're just not going to get it. Moreover, when you require that young kids—those between about six and eight—give to a cause or collection they don't understand or don't really want to give to, you risk the fact that they effectively write off the contribution mentally. Here's what I mean: You pay your daughter an allowance of $3 a week, but you require that she drop $1 into the church collection plate. She doesn't want to do this, but you require it. Fine, she agrees. But here's what's happening inside her head: She's discounting her *real* allowance to $2 and mentally discounting the relevance of that third dollar. It was never money she had any control over to begin with, so it's money that doesn't really exist. It's really Mom and Dad's money, because they're dictating its use.

To counter this, allow her to accumulate the prescribed amount of money in the Giving jar, then help her find a charity to which she feels good about giving. In doing so, you're engaging her in the process of charitable donation; you're helping her learn how to research issues she cares about; and you're allowing her to give her money to something that makes her feel good about herself and her deeds. That's the way to build inside your child a charitable heart that will last a lifetime.

Not every parent will agree with this sentiment, but just as you must generally allow your children to spend their money on the expenses they deem important, you should allow them to donate to causes they deem important. And once your kids become teens, their charitable choices might conflict with your personal leanings. To pick an extreme example (and please don't read any ulterior message into this), a teenaged daughter might decide that supporting Planned Parenthood is the highest use of her charitable dollars, even though her parents are pro-life. That's clearly a conflict. Nevertheless, if a teen can make a cogent argument for why she wishes to support a specific, legitimate cause, then by and large parents should let her. That doesn't mean parents can't explain why they don't support that same cause; indeed, parents should explain their counter stance, calmly and rationally, so that teens can weigh the arguments on both sides of the divide.

The best teachers are those who educate and then encourage students to apply the knowledge to their own path. That applies equally to parents teaching their kids about charity.

Spending: Into the Spending jar goes all the money allocated to buying toys and treats.

This money can be used for whatever your child fancies—again, so long as that fancy fits with the framework of your family's principles. The money can be spent all at once or, as you'll see with that fourth jar, saved for a larger purchase. Resist the urge, however, to impose your tastes or financial values. You might think that spending $20 on collectible trading cards of mythical and imagined monsters is wasteful, but if your child doesn't, that's his choice, and he needs to feel that his money serves his wants. His value system will change over time, just be patient and let him learn by spending as he sees fit.

That doesn't mean you can't offer guidance. You can and should. Help him understand the value of the sum he has to spend. Kids get excited in the moment when there's a new purchase on the horizon, but then feel a sense of buyer's remorse, often within minutes, when they realize that what they bought isn't what they thought it would be, or when they see that they've spent all their money on one item. Play devil's advocate before the purchase: "Are you going to be OK not having any money left after you buy this item?" "What happens if you don't like it and you've spent all your money—will you be upset?"

Explain the consequences: "Once you buy this and open the package, you can't bring it back if you're not happy with it. So be sure this is really what you want." Or, "Remember, this item you're buying is going to cost all the money you have (or half the money, or whatever the case is), so you're not going to be able to buy something else for a while."

Either way let the decision happen as your child chooses. Mistakes will certainly be made. Your role when they occur is to play the supportive, understanding parent—and don't say, "I told you so." Instead, say something like, "Gosh, I'm really sorry this happened; I was worried that it might. I know you must feel bad. Maybe we should use this as a learning experience, and next time think about it a little longer before you make a decision. What do you think?"

At the end of the day, you're on your child's team, not the opponent's. His pain is your pain, and this is not your opportunity to show that you're so much smarter because you're an adult. Particularly in down moments, your aim should be to hold your kids up, help them see their mistakes, and remind them that you're there to guide them through moments like this.

Now, about that fourth jar . . .

Future Spending: When your boss hands you your paycheck (or, possibly, when your company directly deposits your paycheck), do you rush out and spend every last penny that day?

Of course not.

You spend some. You save some (right?). And you keep some

in your checking or savings account for future spending needs, be they needs that you know will arise next week or a couple months from now. That's the way the world really works, and kids need to experience that rather than some simplistic notion of it. After all, kids always have those longer-term wants, though they don't see them that way. In their eyes, their wants are always immediate. My son, for instance, decided one day when he was 11 years old that he really needed an Xbox 360 video game console. He didn't have enough money available at the moment he decided on this want, and a single allowance payment certainly wasn't going to suffice, either. So, he decided the best course of action was to inform his mom and me of this immediate need. Nice try, we told him, and reminded him that this was a perfect example of the type of expense for the fourth jar.

The overriding rule here is that that while your child is certainly free to dump her entire Spending allocation into the Future Spending jar, she cannot contribute money earmarked for the Saving or Giving jar. Once the Future Spending goal has been reached, your child is free to buy the item.

The reason for this fourth jar is revealed in the way parents typically employ the three-jar scheme that requires kids to earmark one third of their money for saving, one third for charity and one third for spending. But think about it. Do you save one third of your paycheck? Do you donate one third of your paycheck? And of the money allocated to spending, do you spend it all at once? True, kids are a special breed, financially speaking. They have no real expenses, so there's certainly an argument to be made that it's okay to impose unrealistic measures upon their finances just to acclimate them to saving and giving.

However, there's an equally good argument for teaching kids how to manage their finances in a more realistic way. Learning to put aside some spending money specifically for later use is clearly one of the lessons that will serve kids well when they're grown. The fourth jar accomplishes that goal, since it focuses a child mentally on tomorrow and the spending desires that will certainly arise.

Yes, you could skip this fourth jar and just let your child save for bigger purchases in the Savings jar, but to a large degree you run up against the same paradox you have with the traditional piggybank: saving just to spend (more on this in Chapter 4). Jar number four alleviates that because it separates core savings from temporary savings. It also sends the clear message that the core savings isn't to be raided for consumer wants, though other savings—temporary savings—can be set aside specifically for certain spending wants that you can't necessarily afford at the moment. Delayed gratification is another beneficial side effect.

As a parent, your aim is to steer your kids to fund the fourth jar with a portion of every allowance payment—a portion of the money allotted to spending—and a portion of every gift of money received on birthdays, holidays and other special events. With this approach, your child can use some of the money for spending on immediate wants right now, if necessary, and still have some money set aside for later.

THE FOURTH-JAR FUNDING FORMULA

As noted a few paragraphs back, parents often opt for the one third/one third/one third recipe when using the three-jar scheme. Four jars would seem to suggest a quarter of every allowance payment should be headed for each jar. Not so, though.

You need to be more realistic, again recognizing that you're trying to teach real-world lessons. As such, instead of divvying the money equally between jars, devote 40% to 50% of the money your child receives to spending, with 10% to 20% of that going to the Future Spending jar. Allocate 10% to 15% to giving, in line with what parents typically give; the rest—35% to 50%—goes into savings.

You might think that 40% to 50% aimed at spending is much too much, particularly given that kids don't have any financial liabilities in their life that their income must cover. But, again, when you're talking about the size of the allowance that most kids earn, and the costs of the items kids want to spend their money on, half an allowance won't go terribly far to begin with. After all, kids aren't pulling in thousands of dollars a year. Even if you pay $10 a week, you're talking about an annual income of just $520, of which your child can spend about $260 between immediate and future wants. Birthday and holiday gifts of cash will increase that to some degree, but even then you're still talking about a relatively small sum of money overall. How far will that money really go, given the cost of the items kids typically want in the modern economy?

Better that your kids feel they have some power to spend a healthy portion of their allowance, otherwise they're not going to pay much attention to their money because they're not going to see that they can do much with their money aside from sticking it into a savings account or donating it to others. Neither is terribly fun for a kid, and, as such, they're not likely to learn many lessons.

How you ultimately decide your children should divvy up their money is entirely a function of your family's values. Some families might emphasize charity over spending on personal wants and thus require that a larger portion go to donations.

Others might emphasize saving, with the idea that they want their children to help afford their own college costs one day.

Finally, to simplify the process of dividing the money between the four jars, pay your child's allowance in denominations that are easily split. If you pay $10 a week, for instance, offering a $10 bill isn't going to help the process much. Pay in singles instead.

THE VACATION BUDGET

One of the best opportunities to teach real-life budgeting happens during family vacations, which serve as microcosms of the everyday spending/saving decisions that are made in the adult world.

Kids love to spend money—Mom and Dad's money—on vacation. They ask to pop into seemingly every souvenir shack the family stumbles upon. But they never think in terms of the financial impact of buying every knickknack they see because the money they're spending isn't theirs and they didn't earn it. So, the spending is painless and meaningless. It's consumption run amok.

There's a better way.

Choose an amount of money you're willing to spend on your kid's souvenir quest, and then a week prior to the vacation announce the amount, but add this caveat: "This is all the money I'm giving you. Spend it all on the first day, and that's it for the rest of the trip. And any amount of money you come home with is yours to keep."

You'll be surprised at how suddenly thoughtful your kid can be when shopping. You likely won't be harassed at every store; your child will comparison shop, will balk at overpriced trinkets, and will return home with money to spare. In short, they will learn how to budget, to stretch their meager sum of dollars across a specific period of time with the aim of having some left over at the end—exactly what an adult budget aims to accomplish.

Just be sure you don't cave in to requests for more money if the sum you allotted is spent before the trip concludes. Doing so will defeat the purpose and send the message that you're an ATM your kids can tap into whenever they run out of cash. Do that enough times and your kids, when they're grown, will have no worries overspending their budget because they will have come to accept that Mom or Dad will bail them out—and you do *not* want to be in that position.

Kid-Sized Credit

Children are not good credit risks.

They are at best sub-prime borrowers: They have little income, they're not employed, and there's a very good chance they're going to welsh on their debt. And *you* are the lender who's going to record the loss. No worries, though. After all, the amount of money kids borrow is generally small. Losing it won't alter your retirement date.

That's not to say, though, that you should just go ahead and loan your kids money whenever they want it, expecting to write off a loss. The lender-borrower relationship will play a big part of every child's adult life, whether it's student loans for college, credit cards, a car loan, a mortgage, a home-equity loan, whatever. You can use their desire to tap your deeper pockets as a learning experience that will shape the way they think about borrowing and debt in the future.

When younger children ask to borrow money—and they will ask—tell them they can have the money, but they have to pay it back, with interest. My son didn't grasp the concept of interest until he was about ten, though some kids will catch on a bit sooner. Either way, when your child eagerly agrees to your proposition, say something like, "Do you understand what you're signing up for?"

What you mean, you tell them, is that if they spend $1, then when you get home, they have to immediately pay you back the $1 from their Spending, Future Spending or Savings jar, plus they have to give you two quarters as the cost of borrowing Mom and Dad's money. Yes, 50% interest is usurious and illegal and most states. But you're running a family on the basis of a benevolent dictatorship, so you can charge whatever fee you like. (I know: I previously said parents can't act dictatorial when teaching money lessons.) In practical terms, you want the borrowing to inflict some measure of financial pain that your kid will feel. Charging a nickel or a dime won't resonate as much as two quarters.

In imposing the fee, explain that this is how it works in the adult world, too, maybe offering an explanation similar to this:

Whenever Mom and Dad borrow money to pay for a house or a car, and sometimes when we use a credit card to buy

*groceries or to take the family to dinner, we have to pay
back all the money we borrowed, plus we have to pay an
additional fee to the bank or credit card company that is
loaning us the money. For you, it means that if you want
to buy a candy bar for $1, you really have to pay $1.50
because you have to pay me back the money you borrowed
plus those extra two quarters as my fee. And, you know,
you could buy half of another candy bar with those two
quarters. The other option is that you can wait until you
have your own money to spend and I will take you to the
store so you can buy your candy bar on your own.*

You're sending two messages: Borrowing to satisfy an immediate craving can be an expensive proposition, and delayed gratification, as noted previously, is a cheaper alternative.

This works best with younger kids with smaller allowances, for whom two quarters really means something. And if your youngster regrets borrowing money to buy something that loses its fun quickly, or if your child realizes he misspent his money and would have rather saved for something more important, don't step in with a bailout, no matter the heartstrings that are tugged. Do so and you begin to establish one of the worst habits—the belief that someone will always step in to repair a financial flub. You know from your own life that's not the case outside that comfortable bubble of childhood, though many, many grown-ups who continually call on Mom and Dad for money never learn that lesson. So don't teach it to your own kids. If a purchase is regrettable, tough. That's a hard lesson to learn, no doubt, but it is one of the most necessary.

When kids are older, in about middle school or so, and definitely once they're in high school, and they seek a parental loan, you can take the next step: a formal loan agreement imposing a more practical, though still meaningful, interest rate.

Older kids have expensive tastes. They're not looking to borrow a dollar to buy a candy bar; they want to borrow hundreds to buy a video game system or new clothes, or a few thousand to buy a car. If you're inclined to offer up the cash, offer up a written agreement, as well, that spells out the terms of the loan. Make it clear that the money is to be repaid monthly, either from an allowance or, with teens who are employed, a part-time job. Impose some interest rate that is meaningful so that, again, your child feels the cost of borrowing.

To emphasize that cost of borrowing, provide a repayment breakdown that shows the true cost of the loan over time. Say your teen borrows $2,000 to buy a used car. You charge 15% interest (yes, still a bit usurious, but, again, benevolent dictatorship) and your child is to repay the loan over two years. That's $96.97 a month (you can easily program Excel or any spreadsheet to calculate this for you with the "payment" function), or $2,327.36 over the life of the loan, meaning, you tell your child, that the loan costs more than $300 in fees—money that otherwise could go to clothes or movies or gas for the car.

To cut those fees, encourage kids to prepay the loan by adding additional principal payments when they receive money for holidays and birthdays. Repaying debt early as a way to trim overall interest costs is one of the smartest financial habits. When your kids are adults paying on a mortgage or a car note, the habit of paying additional principal each month or even once a year can save tens of thousands of dollars or more.

How to handle missed payments is your call. You could impound the car until the past-due amount is paid, but that might impact your own life negatively, since now you or your spouse are on the hook for toting the kids to school, extracurricular activities, and the like. Although, do this one time and there's a pretty good chance your child will never again be late on the payment, since life without a car is perhaps the harshest of punishments for a teenager. The other, less Draconian, measure is to charge an additional fee of $25 for a late payment, similar to the punitive actions of a financial institution. Just be sure to spell out those details in the contract, and highlight them—as in, underline them with a colored marker—so that your child clearly understands the penalty.

Both parties, parent and child, should sign the document, and leave it in a highly visible location, like the refrigerator or a family bulletin board, so that the contract serves as a constant reminder of a loan obligation due on the first of every month.

A Child's First Checking Account

Clearly, younger kids don't need a checking account. So this section really only applies to teens.

The first question to answer is whether your child even needs a checking account. From a logistical standpoint, the answer is yes. Even in an age of electronic payments, you need an account from which money is debited to pay for purchases not settled with cash. From an operational standpoint, the answer is maybe. What costs does your teen have? If the only expenses are trips to the movies, putting gas in a car, buying some clothes every now and then, and spending on a few discretionary wants here and there, then there's probably little need for a checking account since a pocketful of cash will suffice.

Checking accounts are as easy to open as savings accounts,

but there is a small consideration: fees. Banks offer all different levels of checking, and they impose all sorts of fees on those accounts based on everything from the number of checks written in a month to the size of the average daily balance. For the most part, banks don't start waiving fees until an account holds at least $1,000, often more. Teens aren't likely to keep that much money in the account, so you'll want to make sure you find a local bank that offers a bare-bones, no-fee, basic checking account. And be sure you and your teen understand the terms of the account, such as the limit on how many checks can be written each month and the fees for using an ATM that belongs to another bank. As with a savings account, you will likely need to cosign on the checking account, which is good because it means you have final say in the event bad things happen.

More so than with a savings account, a checking account requires that parents talk to their teens about the inherent responsibilities. A once-popular bumper sticker reflective of the shop-till-you-drop mind-set held that "I can't be out of money. I still have checks!" Mildly humorous on a car bumper, not so funny when your son or daughter bounces a check or three for failing to keep track of the account balance. As a parent, you must emphasize to teens that they must:

  a. record accurately and in a timely fashion every
     deposit made, check written and all ATM transac-
     tions and debit expenses;
  b. balance the account every month so that they have
     an accurate picture of their money;
  c. recognize that checks don't move at the speed
     of cash, so that a bank balance online might not

accurately reflect the amount of money in the account;

d. realize that if you overspend your balance, the
bank will not only ding you $25 or more for an
overdraft charge, but the merchant who suffers
from your bounced check will penalize you financially as well.

The inviolable rule you must impose as a parent is that
Mom and Dad retain *complete* access to the account records
online at all times. That means you must always know the
log-in/password information. With online access, you can see
how much money your child is spending and where (and you
should always question the outlays you don't immediately recognize), and how much money remains in the account at any
given point. Your teen might gripe, as teens do, when they per-
ceive that Mom or Dad challenges the unfettered freedom they
think they deserve. But, again, tough noogies. A parent's role
of teacher is subservient to the role of protector. As part of the
account-opening process, make clear to your child that your
interest in the account isn't to say what can and can't be purchased, and you're not going to impose your wishes over the
money, but you do need to make sure that others aren't taking
advantage of your child and that your child is managing the
account properly.

Credit Cards for Kids
. . . .

I'll bet many a parent has heard a comment similar to one
my son made when he was much younger and wanted me to

buy him something at a toy store. I told him, "I don't have any money, buddy."

"You don't need money," he replied. "You have that card in your wallet you used to pay for lunch."

He had a point.

In a modern life, we parents can't help but use credit cards. They're convenient, they're easily (too easily?) obtained, and they're accepted in just about every single place you would otherwise need cash. They're clearly necessary for purchasing goods online, as so many of us do in an Internet age.

Kids see all this happen, though we don't necessarily think about it. Yet the swiping and signing we do numerous times in a week—paying for gas, groceries, dinner at a restaurant, movies, clothes, the plunger at Home Depot, new school supplies, the list is never-ending—registers with our children. They learn by default, and we shouldn't be surprised when they want a credit card of their own at some point.

Many parents will balk at the idea of handing a credit card to their teenager, rightfully fearful of the next monthly statement. But if you teach your kids how the system works, they can learn to be prudent employers of credit. Again, this is one of those lessons better learned in the protective cocoon of home, rather than when they're off on their own, when overspending on credit can cause real financial headaches in their early adult years.

If they make it to college but haven't by then learned about credit cards and the potential destruction a simple piece of plastic can bring, they face some potentially trying financial times. Indeed, consider these statistics from a survey of undergraduate university students by Nellie Mae, a student loan company: 56% of students say they applied for their first credit card as college freshmen and, by their senior year, had accumulated an average balance approaching $3,000; one in 12 students exceeds a balance of $7,000. More than half carry four or more cards. Forty-four percent always carry a balance over from one month to the next, and one in 10 students makes less than the minimum payment due on one or more cards. As you might well imagine, that's not good.

The ultimate result: More graduates entering their working careers are already carrying a debt load, which, in turn, pushes an increasing number of young adults toward bankruptcy.

Schools do little to teach kids personal finance, and credit card applications on a college campus are more prevalent than keg parties. Today's kids—and many of their parents—have grown up in a country where prosperity is widely evident and where all you have to do to have whatever you want is sign on a dotted line. Credit has allowed people to pretend they're prosperous and to forget the hard work and effort that should come first. As such, college students and young adults see that credit cards can effectively buy the life their income otherwise can't afford, a powerful drug when everyone else around you is living large. The end result is that college graduates—and, really, many Americans in general—too often survive just at the brink of financial disaster, one or two paychecks shy of ruin.

Look no further than the debt-induced economic crisis that defined 2007 and 2008, and that pushed the U.S. economy into a funk not seen for decades. That was fueled in large measure by easy credit offered to individuals who ultimately did not understand the financial products they were committing to, particularly complex home mortgages. In turn, that led to credit card defaults and record foreclosures as financially over-extended families learned in harsh terms that their comprehension of personal finance was sorely inadequate.

Understanding credit cards is a key preventive. And what better time to inoculate the mind against the disease of chasing faux prosperity than when it is young and impressionable? That's where a kid-sized credit card comes in handy.

How young? A good time to start is when kids reach high school. That's the age when they're running around the mall and heading off to movies with their friends, and when they have a variety of expenses for school. Some of those are expenses they should manage on their own credit cards.

Certainly, I'm not advocating you sign up your son or daughter for an American Express card and turn them loose. Nevertheless, a credit card with a low credit limit of $100 or $200, or even a debit card tied to a child's personal bank account, is a fine way to teach the good, the bad and the disastrous that all credit cards represent.

Explore your local banks, or look online, and you will find several institutions that offer kid-friendly financial products. Many will allow you to open a bank account and tie a debit card to it, though not all will offer credit cards to kids. Online you'll find a few companies—including PayJr.com—that offer credit cards specifically built for teens, or, more specifically, the parents who want to teach their teens about credit card financing before losing them to the real world.

For parents, these accounts provide online access so that you and your child can check the balance at any given moment, or so that you can monitor your child's spending activity.

Essentially, you have four options for providing your child with a credit/debit card:

1. **Prepaid credit card.** With these, Mom or Dad preloads the card each month with a predetermined amount of

money. When the card is empty, the spending, by necessity, stops. Not a bad option for parents who want to ease a child into a regular credit card. The pitfall: Banks generally impose a variety of fees for services such as reloading the card. And be aware that some merchants' systems don't accept payment from a prepaid card.

2. **Debit card tied to a checking or savings account.** A kid's purchase is directly subtracted from the underlying account. You'll have no worries about usurious interest rates or paying a monthly bill or dings to a credit report if you miss a payment, because there are no payments to miss. However, the account must have an adequate amount of money on deposit, otherwise your child is hit with overdraft charges if he overspends his bank balance. That means debit cards are best when kids have shown an ability to keep their checking/ savings account properly balanced each month, and for those who have shown that they pay attention to how much they're spending.

3. **Adding your child as an authorized user on your existing card.** Credit card companies regularly allow you to do this. The benefits are that you maintain control of the account and are responsible for paying the bill every month instead of leaving it to your child to remember. As such, if your child misses a payment to you, it doesn't show up on her credit report. But that's also the downside: If your little spender goes wild and can't afford to pay you the full amount owed, that could mean you must carry a balance going forward if you don't have the cash yourself to make a full pay-

ment. Therefore, if your child is just spending without thinking about managing the payment, this approach doesn't always teach your child the valuable lessons you hope.

4. **Cosigning for a card specifically for your child.** In terms of education and impact on future finances, this is arguably the best option—but it comes with serious potential for disaster. The card and all the charges and payments become your child's responsibility. As such, a separate card is a very effective, sink-or-swim way to teach concepts of budgeting, wise spending, policing your own charges, and paying off the debt each month. Moreover, with this approach kids begin building their own credit history and credit score—and assuming they manage the card smartly, strong credit scores will help them obtain favorable rates when they seek a car loan or mortgage after college. The downside: Kids can just as easily mismanage their card and rack up a balance they cannot repay, and, because you cosigned, the debt falls onto your shoulders. That could negatively impact your credit scores, leading to higher rates when you seek other consumer loans. And because lenders monitor your credit history closely, a credit score impaired by your child's financial negligence could even push interest rates higher on your other credit cards that aren't tied to your kids.

Regardless of which approach you ultimately choose, be sure to state clearly to your child that you—the parent—will *always* have access to the account so that you can police the purchasing patterns. A debit card must be properly balanced every month, and a credit card balance must be entirely repaid every month. Failure to do so gets us to another Kids & Money rule:

Kids & Money Rule #7: Failure to balance the monthly debit card bank account statement means losing access to the debit card for a week or more; failure to repay an entire month's credit card balance means the loss of the card until the balance is fully paid, plus one additional month.

Of course, with debit cards there's often little reason to balance a checkbook register anymore because the transactions are posted online so quickly it's easy to check your bank balance using the web browser on a mobile phone. Nevertheless, kids need to learn the habit of tracking their income and spending.

As noted several paragraphs back, giving a debit/credit card to kids works best with high school–aged children for several reasons. First, they're generally mature enough mentally to understand that a credit card is simply a replacement for checks or cash (though you might have to explain that explicitly at first). And they typically recognize that the money spent has to be repaid (though, again, you might explicitly detail that fact early on in the process, just to be sure the message resonates). Further, they often shop for clothes and school supplies without Mom and Dad tagging along, or they head to the mall or the movies or on vacations with friends. A debit or credit card gives them access to their cash, but forces them to make the same, hard financial decisions that adults make: Do I really need to spend $110 on another pair of sneakers and deplete my bank account, or can I get by with a $40 pair that leaves me some money to do other things with my friends? Given that choice, teens will often enough make the financially savvy decision to trade down in order to preserve their cash for other wants and needs.

But here's the big caveat: Don't just hand over a piece of financial plastic and expect that through use your child will learn about the wise application of credit. The Jump$tart Coalition for Personal Financial Literacy found that when questioned about how credit cards work, one-third of kids who use credit cards—either their own or their parents'—scored worse than peers who didn't have access to a credit card. As such, if you plan to provide your child with any type of credit or debit card, you must also provide some education as well.

Key points they need to understand are:

- Credit cards are *not* Monopoly money. You're spending real dollars when you sign the receipt, and that means you must repay real dollars from your own bank account when the credit card bill arrives each month.
- Credit cards impose an interest rate for gaining access to money you don't have in your wallet at the moment.
- The interest rate is typically among the highest in the financial-services industry.
- If you pay only the minimum payment due each month and don't pay off your entire balance, the credit card company adds an interest charge to your outstanding balance, meaning you owe more than you've

actually charged. This is basically the negative version of compounding interest in a savings account, only now you're compounding your costs.

- A credit card means you necessarily have a credit report, and credit reports follow you throughout your lifetime. So if you skip payments because you don't have the money, or because you forgot, or because you wanted to use that money instead to buy or do something else, your credit report will display that to every other lender who ever considers loaning you money for a car or a house or another credit card—and that will impact your financial life for years.

Illustrate some of these points with an actual example: Allow your teen in the first month to charge $50 and then pay just the minimum when the bill arrives. In the second month, allow your child to charge another $50. When the second bill arrives, point out the interest charge that the credit card company will have added to the balance due. Sure, the charge won't be terribly high on such a small balance. Nevertheless, it clearly underscores your message that if every month you charge more than you can afford to repay, and then allow that balance to roll over to the next month, you will reach a point where even the minimum payment stretches your financial abilities—and that's where consumers get into financial distress that leads to bankruptcy.

In general, credit and debit cards aren't appropriate for middle school children. At that age, kids are still too young and need more time handling real money before they start using the virtual money that a credit card represents. Moreover, aside from wanting money to buy some video game or whatnot, most middle schoolers aren't too occupied with money, so dumping even a prepaid credit card in their lap isn't very helpful.

However, there might be one exception. Middle school and older elementary-aged kids are often big fans of kid-friendly online gaming communities (such a Club Penguin, run by Disney; or those run by Nickelodeon's nickjr.com), where they play and chat with their peers over the Internet. Many such sites, like those run by Disney and others, impose monthly subscription charges of between $5 and $10. In this instance, a debit card can be a fine way of teaching a financial lesson.

In this case, tie a debit card to a child's savings account (if your bank allows that) or use one of the online sites that provides a debit card tied to an account that you fund with the routine allowance payments. Your child then can use the debit card to pay the gaming community subscription. This strategy forces kids to think about whether this gaming community is really so important, and it requires them to pay very close attention to how much they're spending. Many online communities offer free versions of their site, enticing kids into the paid portion by promising access to other virtual worlds or better virtual loot. But the free site might be good enough for some kids who decide they might want to spend their limited cash resources elsewhere.

No matter the age, if you provide your child with a credit or debit card, you must teach the necessity of tracking spending every month so that charges and debits do not exceed the month's income or the balance available in the underlying account. One way to accomplish this is the simple but effective "tick-off" method. On a piece of paper—and graph paper works well for this—draw a series of squares equal to the amount of money your child receives each month in allowance. Each box represents $1. So, if you pay your son $10 a week, then there are 40 boxes on the page (this is why graph paper works so well; the boxes are already drawn and you just have to label them appropriately).

With each dollar spent, the appropriate number of boxes is ticked. This way, kids know exactly how much they've already committed themselves to repaying on their credit card, or how much has already come out of their account on the debit card, and that can help prevent overspending.

4

. . . .

Saving

LAYING THE CORNERSTONE OF
FINANCIAL SECURITY

If learning to spend prudently is, as I wrote in the previous chapter, one of the most important building blocks of personal finance, then learning to save some of what you otherwise would spend is the cornerstone. Saving is perhaps the single most significant financial life skill parents can teach to children. The benefits will provide the lifetime of financial security that comes from having physical dollars in the bank and the peace of mind those dollars represent.

That was a lost lesson for much of the past couple of decades as America binged on gluttonous consumerism. Big TVs. Big houses. Big sport utility vehicles. As one of the popular catchphrases of the time succinctly encourages: Go big . . . or go home. With $14 trillion in household debt as of 2009—the equivalent of nearly $46,000 per person, the world's largest consumer debt load—Americans clearly went big.

Too big, it turned out.

Once the world's largest creditor nation and home to consummate savers who regularly squirreled away between 7% and 10% of their disposable income, the United States transformed into the world's largest debtor nation. By the early 1990s, the savings rate plunged, spending soared, and credit exploded as consumers increasingly tapped credit cards or the equity in their homes to live an aspirational lifestyle. When the crash came in 2008 and 2009, many of those households were unprepared for the destruction.

Some good came of the meltdown, though. Chastened by the imploding bubble of debt and worried about the worst economy to wash across the country since the Great Depression of the 1930s, Americans began to reacquaint themselves with the forgotten wisdom of saving. In late 2008, the nation's savings rate, which had been bouncing around at less than 1% of income for four years, began to surge. By early 2009, Americans were saving almost 5% of their income. Putting money in the bank has returned to the forefront, though how long that trend ultimately lasts is uncertain.

At its core, savings is about thrift, or managing money circumspectly. You don't spend just because you have the money to spend. You buy what you must, but you save what you must as well, because as the sour economy sadly demonstrated, you never know what financial challenge tomorrow might bring.

For today's youth, in particular, tomorrow could be particularly challenging. Corporate pension plans have long been on the way out, replaced by the now-ubiquitous 401(k) retirement-savings plan. But even those aren't certain to survive. During the recession that began in 2007, companies including FedEx, Eastman Kodak, Motorola, General Motors, Ford Motors and Resorts International, among others, all canceled company contributions to workers' 401(k) accounts. The move might prove temporary, or it might not. And then there are the widely reported struggles facing the Social Security system, which will impact today's kids when they reach retirement age. Don't take my word for it; the Social Security website, in a Q&A section, clearly warns that unless changes are made soon—and political will never seems abundant enough to do *that*—benefits for workers who retire in 2041 could be reduced by 22%, and future benefits could be cut even more. (By the way, 2041 would mark the retirement date for people born in 1974—people who are already raising kids of their own!)

So why, some might be wondering right now, do I mention all of this bleak information in a chapter on teaching kids to save?

Isn't it obvious?

The children who are raised with a healthy grasp of saving, who learn to live with thrift as a guiding force, and who religiously save a portion of every paycheck are going to be better able to cope with the challenges America will face in the future.

Kids are natural savers. At early ages you see that in little ways unrelated to money. Some kids instinctively save various knickknacks, whether they are stickers or trading cards or Barbie dolls. These instincts don't necessarily migrate over to dollars as kids age, so it's during this time that you want to engage them. After all, on some level saving is nothing more than collecting money. If you wait until they grow more accustomed to spending than saving, it will be harder to instill that savings mentality. They won't necessarily see money in reserve as a good thing; they're just as likely to see it as a missed spending opportunity.

Though many families struggle with saving, it's not so terribly hard to do, really—though it can require a mind-set shift.

In physical terms it's no different than spending. You are allocating part of your discretionary income to a particular cost, and in this case that cost is buying financial security. Instead of buying consumer junk by spending that money at a store, you effectively "spend" your money buying a bank account.

Mentally, however, saving is an entirely different game. That's where the big problem lays for so many parents and, by extension, so many kids. Kids are a reflection of Mom and Dad, a mirror showing us exactly who we are as parents—the good and the not so good. If you openly worry about money, your kids are prone to worry about money. To get kids moving toward a healthy savings ethic, we have a few strategies to employ. And we'll start with, perhaps, the oldest child-friendly savings strategy around—but with a twist.

Piggybanks

The pig-shaped bank so many people associate with childhood has been around for eons. One tale of the piggybank's rise holds that metal was too expensive in the Middle Ages and that a type of clay, called pygg, was commonly used to fashion pots for cooking and jars. Families, particularly poorer families without access to a banking system built largely for the aristocracy, commonly used one of the pygg jars—a pygg bank—to hold the family's coins. From that grew the piggybank . . . or at least that's one theory.

Whatever the case, kids love piggybanks—if only because they sort of resemble a toy, and they can provide a certain level of enjoyment. So make one a central component of your child's early savings efforts. In fact, if you care to lead by example, keep your own adult version of a piggybank—whether an empty mayonnaise jar or some other big bottle—in a highly visible spot right next to your child's piggybank, and then encourage your child to save by making a point of contributing spare change to your own piggybank regularly.

As the coins mount, spend time helping your child count the money that has amassed. You might do this monthly to match a bank's statement cycle, but more likely you want to let a couple of months pass so that your child has time to accumulate enough coins to make the effort educational. Keep a piece of paper stuffed in the piggybank that shows the increasing balance over time, a visual indicator that saving regularly grows your wealth. If your child plans to spend the money on a particular want, make note of the cost on that same piece of paper. As the balance in the pig rises, decrease the amount still needed to afford the purchase on the other side of the ledger. Your child will begin to see the cause-and-effect relationship between saving over time and ultimately being able to afford something you want.

But piggybanks have some inherent weaknesses. First, piggybanks offer no rate of return, so they are effectively dead money (though that's not such a great sin, given that piggybanks are about learning, not earning). Second, we all have in our mind that image of a hammer cracking open the pig to gain access to the money for some discretionary want. Indeed, as the example in the previous paragraph points out, parents often use piggybanks as a way to get kids to save just to the point that they accumulate enough money to go buy something they've been yammering for. That sends the unfortunate message that the only reason you save is so that you can spend—and that's not a financially savvy message.

Such shortcomings are easily managed, though.

Add a rate-of-return to piggybank savings by offering interest on the money your child maintains in the piggybank at the end of each month. Incorporate this "interest payment" into the process of routinely helping your child calculate the sum of money inside the pig. After you two have added up all the coins and bills, add your stated contribution before recording the ending value for the month. Since this is a strategy geared mainly at younger kids, you don't need a real interest rate. Instead, just agree to add some particular amount of money to the piggybank each month that your child maintains a balance. That might be an agreement to match some level of money in the piggybank, or maybe you opt to contribute a few quarters of your own or a dollar bill. Whatever the case, make it an amount that excites your child. You'll know the right amount just by paying attention to your child's reactions when you deposit the money. Be upbeat about the procedure; kids feed off Mom and Dad's joy, so if you make a big deal about adding a crisp dollar bill to the piggybank, your kids will come to think of it is a big deal, too.

There's no need to explicitly detail this idea of *interest*, because that's likely a bit much for young kids. They will assuredly grasp, however, that they're receiving extra money just for letting their coins sit untouched in the bank. And you can use that experience later when it comes time to open a real bank account for your kids and you're trying to explain how interest works. The piggybank experience will make interest immediately understandable.

As for dealing with the save-to-spend issue, all you have to do is stipulate that only a portion of the money can be spent, that the pig's belly can never go empty.

Kids & Money Rule #8: Only 50% of the money put into a piggy-bank can be taken out to buy something. At least half must remain inside the pig.

Also, the next time money is removed, the value of the money remaining in the pig must be larger than the balance left after the last time money was withdrawn. In other words, a child with $10 in the piggybank can spend $5, but if after doing so he happens to save another dollar (resulting in a $6 piggybank balance), he can't decide to now withdraw $3, or half the remaining balance, for another purpose. That strategy just defeats the purpose of saving since he's just slowly draining the account. If he adds $1, the most he can withdraw is 50 cents so that $5.50 remains in the account.

By insisting that the current balance never dip below the balance remaining at the last withdrawal, you're helping ensure that your child has an ever-growing savings account, while at the same time teaching him to pay attention to his savings and, equally important, the size of his spending demands. (This is a good reason, by the way, to keep that piece of paper tucked inside the pig that keeps the running balance. You won't have to rack your brain trying to remember how much remained after the last withdrawal.)

Before moving on, let me digress to acknowledge that I realize much of this—charging interest, paying interest, drawing up loan agreements with your kids, counting coins with your kids—it all sounds like a huge strain on your time. It's not. You're just seeing all the components compressed into a single book, and by reading this you're contemplating all the

possibilities in one block. In reality, once you begin to implement the various ideas you'll realize that it's not consuming a
great deal of time, because you won't be doing everything at
once. All of these exercises are part of a progression of teaching your kids over time.

Save and Match

I'm going to repeat some version of this concept in various
places in this book, and the reason is because the underlying principle represents an effective tool for encouraging kids
to save. Over time, implanting this savings ethic is crucial to
financial self-sufficiency and financial security as an adult.
The concept is simple: When it comes to helping your child
save, whether in a piggybank, a bank savings account or even
a 401(k) or IRA when your teen lands a job, pony up some of
your own money to match all or a portion of whatever amount
your child contributes to the account.

You can apply this program in two ways: to encourage core
savings, or to assist your child in reaching a short-term savings
goal sooner. Either way, the strategy is the same: For every bit
of money your child stashes away, agree to match some portion
of it, much like an employer matches a worker's contributions in
a 401(k) retirement-savings plan. If your young daughter saves
$2 from her allowance, for instance, then add another 50 cents
or $1 to the balance.

By adding additional money to a core savings account, you
are putting your money where you mouth is, so to speak. In
contributing to your child's account, your actions reinforce your
words that saving is important.

As for helping a child reach a short-term saving goal, you are sending the message that sometimes people have to save before they can spend, but you're making the process easier for your child, since kids aren't wired for waiting. Make your daughter wait too long before she can buy what she's jonesing for, and her interest in saving is sure to wane; it will seem pointless because she'll believe that it's impossible to reach her goals. When you do add money to a sum your child is saving for a particular spending desire, you want the inducement to be big enough that your child recognizes it as a benefit, but not so large that it becomes a way that she can rely on you to reach her goal for her. So, for instance, when your little girl asks you to top up the sum of money she has available at the moment to buy something she otherwise can't afford, say "no" and explain that when a price tag exceeds your current means, then you can't buy the item immediately. That doesn't mean you can never buy the item, only that you'll have to buy it later, once you have enough money to pay the costs. This is when you offer the "save and match" incentive to encourage her to save.

As part of this matching program, first help her calculate how long it will take to save the required amount based on how much money she currently has and how much she expects to earn from her allowance. Then calculate how long it will take to save the required sum with your contribution factored in. With younger kids—those between roughly five and eight years old—you don't want the wait to stretch too far beyond a few weeks. Otherwise, the exercise is counterproductive to your lesson. Such a wait will feel interminable, and kids will lose interest in the item and grow frustrated. They will instead decide that they should have just bought what they wanted when they wanted it for fear of never getting it. As kids age, the length of time required for saving the necessary money can stretch to several weeks. With older kids, those well into their teens, the wait can extend to several months if needed.

Ultimately, this situation isn't really about the incentive money you offer. Honestly, you could have just handed over the needed sum at the time of the request and you would have spent the same amount. Instead, it's about kids learning to delay gratification and put forth an effort to save money until they can afford their wants. This is a core tenet of financial self-sufficiency as an adult, when you can't run to Mom and Dad every time you see something you want to buy but can't afford (too many adult children already do that, to their own detriment and to the detriment of their aging parents, and too many parents enable the activity). As an added benefit, your child will gain a sense of financial accomplishment that will boost her self-confidence with money, saving and spending as an adult.

When your daughter finally accumulates the necessary savings, offer options. Tell her she can go to the store to buy the item she has been saving for. Or, now that she knows how much effort goes into accumulating larger sums of money, tell her she can opt to save all or part of the money instead of spending it. Some kids will choose the purchase; some will choose to save; some will split the middle, buying something smaller while saving the rest. Whatever option she chooses be excited and congratulate her on having the patience to save for something that was really important. *Do not* belittle the purchase by implying that it's a waste of all the money your child has saved, and don't try to talk her out of spending her money on what she saved for. Kids have to know that it's okay to spend and that there is a reward at the end of all the hard work. Otherwise, you are undermining confidence and eroding your child's independence, which over time can create an adult who either rebels and is reckless with money, or who becomes financially subservient to a spouse.

My First Real Savings Account

At some point, piggybanks and jars just aren't enough. While they will remain a useful means for saving and allocating money for different purposes well into a child's early teens, a real savings account is in order at some point. A traditional savings account either at a local bank or online will not only acclimate your youngster to the basics of banking, it will put your child's money to work earning real interest instead of faux interest from Mom and Dad.

Consider opening a savings account in your child's name within the first year of life, assuming you've applied for a Social Security card, which you should do while filling out the necessary paperwork for a birth certificate. Certainly, your infant won't have any need to go to the bank for several years, so in the interim just deposit into this account the birthday and holiday checks that friends and relatives will undoubtedly send. You'll want to begin introducing your child to this account, and encouraging saving in this account, by about age six. You can explain that all the money currently in the account is money sent by friends and relatives through the years, and, oh, isn't it cool how this money has added up to such a big number over time?

Many local banks and credit unions offer a kid-friendly savings account, often called a Young Savers Account. Some will offer an above-market interest rate, a bonus deposit of $10 or so just for opening the account, and a periodic newsletter written for kids. If you feel comfortable online, consider a web-based bank such as ZionsDirect.com, INGDirect.com, EverBank.com or EmigrantDirect.com. They won't necessarily have kid-specific accounts, but parents can still open an account in their child's name. The benefit of an online savings account is that it generally offers far fatter interest rates than you'll find at the local bank. As of early 2009, several online banks were offering interest rates as high as 3%, while local banks were well below 0.5%. Money in online banks is just as safe as money in a local branch, since the online bank deposits are covered by the same Federal Deposit Insurance Corp. (FDIC) guarantee that protects your money on deposit at a local bank.

Since kids can't legally sign binding contracts, you will have to open the account for your child, usually as an UGMA or UTMA (Uniform Gift to Minors Act; Uniform Transfers to Minors Act). These accounts effectively mean the money on deposit is for the benefit of the child, not the parents or guardian. As such, there are certain legal stipulations and tax-related issues that might require you to check in with a trusted lawyer or accountant.

If you decide to wait until your child is older to open a real savings account, whether online or at the neighborhood bank, involve your child in the process. Explain why you're making this choice—that money in the bank is safer than money sitting in a piggybank or jar at home; that the money is accessible whenever needed; and that the bank will pay interest, just like the money Mom and Dad have been contributing each month. Be mindful of the words you choose to describe a bank and a savings account, because kids think in literal terms—and the literal definitions of some words can raise concern in a child's mind. For instance, you *don't* want to announce that a savings account is safe because the money is "locked up." To a kid, "locked up" effectively means prison, and prison means you can't get out, and at the banking level that must mean his money can't get out, even if he wants it. Kids don't want to think that their money is inaccessible. Instead, note that the money is safe, that it won't ever be lost, that no one else can touch it, and that the child can walk into the bank any day he wants (or go online anytime, as the case may be) to take the money back out if he wants to.

When the first few statements arrive, spend a few minutes going over them with your child, showing how the month started with the beginning balance, and how it ended with the ending balance, and all the deposits and withdrawals that took place during the month that determined that ending balance. Focus specifically on the interest payment, noting that it is the money the bank is paying you, the saver, to keep your money there. As the account balance grows, compare the most recent interest payment to previous months, pointing out that the interest payment is getting bigger and bigger. This is a good moment to stress that these larger interest payments represent "money at work"—your dollars are generating more dollars even if you do nothing because the interest you received in earlier months is now earning its own interest.

Every few weeks, or as the situation warrants, take your child to the bank to deposit whatever savings have accumulated in the piggybank or the core Savings jar. Encourage your child to fill out the deposit slip and to hand it to the teller. It's not a big lesson, but it gets your child accustomed to dealing with banks. Clearly this isn't an option with an online bank, though you can re-create some semblance of it by including your child in the online transfer process. (Most online banks generally tie your online account to an account at a hometown bank; that way you can easily transfer money back and forth online. As such, you might still need to open an account in your child's name at a local bank, or just deposit the funds in your local account and then transfer the money to your child's online account.)

Whose Account Is This, Anyway?

In every parent's life there will come a point when your child will utter these words, possibly verbatim: "But I have money in my bank account! And I can spend what I want."

This assertion will almost always arise just after you've nixed some particular spending request, typically at a moment when your child doesn't have enough cash on hand but recognizes that a veritable treasure chest sits unused in the savings account. If I have money in the bank, a kid will rationally conclude, then that's my money and I should be able to take it out to buy what I want.

You can't argue with the logic without being a hypocrite, because it's the same logic every parent uses when pulling their own money out of savings to pay for something. Of course, there is this niggling fact: Parents know best, and we realize that yanking money out of your savings for every passing fancy is a certain path to financial ruin. Kids, of course, don't know that. All they know is that there's money in their account and they want to go to the bank.

And you don't want them to.

So whose account is this, anyway?

As a parent, you might reflexively think you're in charge,

that you have a responsibility to protect kids from making mistakes—and you see draining a savings account for some discretionary purchase as a clearly defined "mistake." And obviously you do own that obligation.

Yet you also owe it to your children to allow them to make financial mistakes at an age when the repercussions of bad decisions have no impact on their financial well-being. Watching your child fritter away money can be painful, particularly when the remorse you know is coming suddenly descends; your child is dejected at having misspent all this money he had been saving for so long; and you have no way to make it better. But better for parent and child to feel miserable now, when the stakes are so low, because when the stakes are magnitudes higher as an adult, the financial damage and the regret can be immensely more debilitating.

So while this might go against all that you believe in personally, kids should be allowed to spend down their savings account—down to zero, if that's what it takes—to learn the lessons of spending cavalierly.

Kids & Money Rule #9: Children should have the right to screw up financially so that they can learn from their mistakes.

As with so many situations, the results of their own actions teach so much more than the words you utter. You will be proven right over time, but until your child experiences just how right you are, your words are whispers in a windstorm. Additionally, in allowing kids the freedom to spend their accounts to zero, you will not face the pouting or arguing or silent treatment that typically goes hand in hand with you denying them access to their bank account. Say yes, and you defuse a conflict before it sparks, and pave the way for one of the most valuable financial lessons: learning to temper your wants.

Other practical reasons exist for allowing kids to pull money from their own savings account. For one, they need to see the full spectrum of banking—that money can come out just as easily as it goes in. Because of the rules parents often assign to children's savings accounts ("this money is for your college" or "this is money for your car one day"), kids in many instances quickly surmise that a bank is little more than a financial black hole into which their money flows, never, it seems, to make the round trip back into their hands.

That roach motel strategy—the money goes in, but it doesn't come out—is understandable, but you risk turning kids off of savings. More important, you may unintentionally encourage financial subterfuge in which your child saves a perfunctory amount according to family standards, but squirrels away money somewhere at home so that cash is available for the expenses that the savings account isn't allowed to cover. You're creating kids who learn to lie about money, a trait that won't fare them well in their own relationships later in life.

Conversely, a kid who knows her savings account isn't off limits for her spending needs is more likely to keep more of her money in the bank, and be comfortable with the fact she can withdraw her money when she wants to make a purchase. It's a bit of reverse psychology in action. Also, if more of her money is in the bank, it's not in her room where she can see it . . . because when kids see money—just like when parents see money in their own wallet—they're much more inclined to feel that burning, universal urge to spend it.

Now none of this means you should encourage your kids to spend their savings account to zero just to teach a lesson. To the contrary, you should always encourage your kids to save, and you should talk to them about the ramifications of pulling money out of savings for a purchase that is probably impulsive to begin with. But if your child insists on spending savings foolishly, go on the record making your case against the purchase. If your warnings thud to the ground, then step back and watch what happens. Some purchases won't prompt regret; some purchases will. And it's those that are most regrettable that will resonate the loudest.

One final note to wrap up this chapter: Always—always— be proud of what your child tries to accomplish, even if the efforts come up short (that goes for so many aspects in life, not just financial). Kids thrive on parental pride and approval and are far more eager to strive toward your goals when they know you'll support them when they succeed and, particularly, when they fail. Announce how proud you are of the effort and offer constructive advice on how to improve next time.

You will boost your child's self-confidence, help him develop valuable saving habits, and, more important to the theme of this book, build an adult who makes smart decisions about money.

Investing

TEACHING KIDS TO PUT THEIR MONEY TO WORK

The stock market might seem an odd topic to cover in a book on kids and money. After all, you don't find many teenage commentators on CNBC, and few kids at Christmas or for birthdays clamor for shares of Microsoft instead of Microsoft's Xbox 360 video game system.

Yet, in terms of rounding out a child's financial education, understanding the stock market at some point is a must. Your goal as a parent is to expose your children to activities that will benefit them throughout their life, and investing for their own future clearly fits that mandate. This is true now more than ever, given that workers are increasingly responsible for their own financial security in retirement. Thus, whether it's handling their own 401(k) retirement-savings plan one day or simply understanding what professional investors are doing on their behalf, you want your children to feel comfortable managing the investment-related issues they will certainly face as adults.

That doesn't mean they need the acumen of a Wall Street research analyst or that you need to read them bedtime stories from *The Wall Street Journal*. Instead, it means kids simply need to be familiar with how investing works and to see for themselves that success as an investor doesn't require an advanced degree in applied mathematics. They need to realize that investing really is a skill that anyone can master no matter a family's financial background and no matter whether they grow up to be a plumber, a lawyer, a nurse or a cabdriver.

To be clear, this chapter isn't going to be a dry recital of complicated discounted cash-flow models and asset-allocation theories. That certainly won't serve you well when it comes to kids. Most people don't much care for that level of financial minutiae themselves, especially when you consider all the daily headaches they're already managing in their lives.

Of course, you very well could be one of the exceptions to this overly broad rule. However, Americans are frequently intimidated by the concept of "Wall Street," a fact borne out in research from retirement-plan giant Fidelity Investments that shows roughly a quarter of all eligible workers don't contribute to a 401(k) plan. Some fail to do so because they don't understand the investment choices in the plan or how to allocate their money. Others are too intimidated by what they see as "high finance," and they don't pursue help because they don't know where to go or what to ask. Of those who do contribute to their plan, a large portion never moves beyond the default investment option their company sticks them in, even though that might be entirely the wrong option for their particular needs.

This chapter instead aims to make investing kid friendly— and parent friendly. The idea isn't to build the next great mutual fund manager but to acclimate children to investing terms and procedures, and to do so in a way that resonates with their way of thinking at a young age.

That means no talk about price-earnings ratios and dividend yields and whatnot with preteen investors. Kids don't understand that; they don't care about it in their narrowly prescribed world of interests, and they're not going to spend the time doing the necessary math. Instead, you're going learn to talk about why some particular company might be a good investment or not, based on what you and your child see happening with your own eyes. In other words, you're going to teach your kids to invest based on their own, very real perceptions about a company they are familiar with either because the family uses the products or shops the stores. It's investing from what Wall Street calls "the bottom-up" approach, or what the rest of us call "kicking the tires."

When to Begin

You've probably seen newspaper stories from time to time about some stock market prodigy who began helping Mom or Dad pick stocks as a seven-year-old. If you have such a child, fantastic; start the learning early. For the average kid, though, you probably want to introduce investing once they've hit sixth or seventh grade.

Younger kids generally aren't focused enough to pay attention to what you're trying to teach, and they'll want to invest in anything you mention just because they think agreeing with you is going to make you happy. If you're an investor yourself, then certainly begin exposing your younger kids to investing by including them in your activities, whether that's researching a stock or mutual fund, or going over your monthly account statement. Heck, inclusion can be something as simple as noting the family's ownership in some company when you pass the store on the road or buy the product at the store. When my son was eight or nine years old, I routinely made a point of mentioning our family's ownership of Kansas City Southern shares every time I saw a KCS train when driving around town. I'd tell him, "We own that train!" He always got excited, and by age 12 he had his own brokerage account and was asking thoughtful questions about what it means to own a stock and why companies pay dividends. And it all started with, "We own that train!"

Such young kids aren't likely to pick up on a whole lot, true. But they're naturally interested in what parents do and generally grow up wanting to emulate Mom and Dad. Thus, you're building their interest for later.

Kids become more discerning as they move through middle school and into high school. Actually, you might be surprised at how perceptive kids can be at picking out trends that are long-lived and fads that aren't. They know quality, as well. They know what they like and what they see that others like. They also have a longer attention span at that age, and a deeper interest in money. This is the time when you want to really focus their attention on Wall Street. Indeed, once kids hit their mid-teens, you can begin introducing more complex concepts such as the price-earnings ratios, dividend yields, and sales-growth figures that investors typically use to measure a stock's worth. However, this isn't even necessary unless your child has real interest. (If that interest does arise, there are many books quite good at explaining these concepts in elegantly simple fashion; I'm partial to *One Up on Wall Street*, by famed Fidelity mutual fund legend Peter Lynch.)

At whatever age you start, remember that this exercise is going to be a show-and-tell process, not just a bunch of talking from you. Words are fine, but the actions you and your child are involved in together will drive home the messages you're trying to teach. So be hands on, and let your kids be hands on, even when that means they choose an investment you otherwise frown on. Just as we learned with spending and saving, remember that the best investing lessons often grow out of failure, and no better lesson exists than to see your money shrivel because of a bad investment rationale.

Finding a Broker

The first step in the learning process is opening a brokerage account in your child's name. Assuming your child is under the so-called age of majority (usually 18 or 21, depending on your state), you'll be opening the account yourself, since kids can't legally sign the necessary contracts. The account, however, belongs to your child. It will either be a Uniform Gift to Minors Act (UGMA) or a Uniform Transfers to Minors Act (UTMA) account.

Every brokerage firm offers these accounts. So your only real concern is finding a low-cost firm from which to operate. Nothing against full-service brokers, but, in this instance, there's no reason to sign on with one of them; the commissions tied to those accounts are generally much too steep, both in real dollar terms and as percentage of the cost of the transaction. Your smartest path is to set up an account with a discount broker offering online trading. The Internet is littered with numerous deep-discount firms, and a quick search will turn up a handful for you to investigate. Two of the better choices are Scottrade.com (a $7 commission as of 2009) and Sharebuilder. com (commission as low as $4 for a basic account). Fidelity, Charles Schwab and E*Trade are fine, too, though their commissions are slightly more expensive.

You can include your child in this process if you want, but, at younger ages, that's not really necessary. Either way, best to have the account open before you start teaching your child about Wall Street so that you have a venue for investing when the two of you begin picking stocks or mutual funds.

Even if your child isn't part of the process of opening the account, let her deposit the money at the firm—in person, assuming you're using a firm with a local office. That's one of the small, but useful, benefits of Scottrade; the firm has storefronts in many cities, meaning you and your child can pop in to deposit money directly or, if you choose, to open the account together in person. For this same reason, Fidelity or Schwab can be good choices, too, despite the added commission costs.

That's not to rule out Internet-only firms. If having your child interact directly with a brokerage firm isn't terribly important to you, or you don't have a local brokerage office in town, then online-only firms can be a just as good a choice. And it's just as easy to involve kids without physically being in an office. Have your child sit with you at the computer, and maybe even delegate keyboard duties to your child whenever you're dealing with the account online.

The initial size of your child's account might also influence your brokerage firm selection. Sharebuilder imposes no minimum amount to open the account. Scottrade requires $500; Fidelity, $2,500. The point is that you should shop around to find the account that best fits all your needs, keeping in mind that the overriding factor should be commissions. You want to pay as little as possible, given what is likely to be the relatively small investments your child will make.

Once the account's open, the fun begins . . .

Stocks, Bonds or Mutual Funds?

If you already know the difference between stocks, bonds and mutual funds, skip this box. If you don't know, or are a bit uncertain, keep reading.

STOCKS: A piece of paper that denotes ownership in the equity of a company. Equity means you share in the profits and losses the company accumulates. You're also entitled to vote on corporate matters and you get a share of any dividends the company pays out.

As a company's business grows bigger through the years, and as it earns increasing amounts of money or pays larger and larger dividends, the value of your stock will generally rise—though that's not always the case, since the underlying U.S. economy can undermine the shares from time to time. As such, stocks are the highest risk, highest reward way to invest in a company. Too many people look at stocks as lottery tickets, but the fact is they are pieces of a business. Buy stocks like lottery tickets and you are destined to win about as often as you win the lottery.

In Kid Terms: You own an ice-pop stand. You get to keep all the money you make from selling ice-pops. You get to decide what flavors you want to sell.

If the summer is really hot and lots of kids in your

neighborhood are buying more and more ice-pops to stay cool, your ice-pop stand earns more and more money, and you get to keep whatever is left after paying for the juices and cups and other supplies to make your ice-pops.

But if the summer months are unusually cool and rainy, your ice-pops might not sell very well. You could end up making very little money, or you might even lose most or all of the original money you spent buying those supplies.

BONDS: A piece of paper that denotes you have loaned money to a company. In effect, you are a lender, just like a bank, and the company in question is in debt to you. During the time the debt remains outstanding, the company sends you interest payments, generally twice a year. After a predetermined number of years, the interest payments stop and the company returns to you the original money you loaned it.

Broadly speaking, bonds function based on three numbers: rate, maturity and face value, all of which are spelled out on the bond itself. Rate is the annual interest rate you will receive; maturity is how the long the bond will exist before the company returns your principal; and face value is the value printed on the face of the bond, or, in other words, what the bond is worth at maturity. Again broadly speaking, bonds tend to be low-risk, low-reward, particularly U.S. government bonds and the bonds of major U.S. corporations.

In Kid Terms: Before summer begins, you loan your best friend at school $30 so he can start his own ice-pop stand. He promises that at the end of each of the three summer months he will pay you $12 so that when the summer is over you have $36, $6 more than you had before. If he can't pay you back because sales are bad, he promises to give you all his ice-pop supplies so that you can sell them and keep whatever money remains.

But you have no say-so in the ice-pop flavors he sells, even if he decides the only flavor he wants to sell is nasty old licorice, and you have no control over how much he charges, even if you think he's charging too much or too little.

If his licorice ice-pops earn tons of money you get back $36. If his licorice ice-pops only earn a little money, you get back $36. Or you could get back less, maybe even nothing. If his licorice ice-pops are so yucky or so expensive that no kids want to buy them, your friend will have no money to repay the loan, and you'll end up with a bunch of licorice-ice-pop supplies that could be hard to sell.

MUTUAL FUNDS: If a stock is an apple and a bond is a kumquat, mutual funds are a fruit salad—a mixture of various investments. Some funds own dozens or hundreds of different stocks in a variety of industries; others own stocks and bonds together; some own just bonds. Whatever the mixture, the aim of a mutual fund is to spread the risk around so that if one stock or one bond explodes, investors aren't hurt as much. Of course, if all stocks or corporate bonds are sinking at the same time, then the mutual fund investor is certainly going to feel the pain.

In Kid Terms: You own an ice-pop stand on one street corner; a hot-dog stand on another street corner that your friend is running for you; you bought a lawnmower for your little brother; and you loaned your sister money to start a Slip 'n Slide water park in the backyard.

You are what investors called "diversified," because you have your money working for you in a bunch of businesses. You're earning money from the ice-pop and hot-dog stands, you're getting part of the money your little brother earns mowing neighborhood lawns, and your sister is repaying with a little bit of interest the loan you gave her for the Slip 'n Slide.

In the best situation, ice-pops and hot dogs are selling well, your brother is cutting several yards a day, and your sister's backyard water park is filled will neighborhood kids from morning to night.

But you're also protected in the event something goes wrong. Maybe it is a cool summer and your ice-pops aren't selling, but at least those warm hot dogs are doing well enough to offset the slow ice-pop sales. And if it's hot but rainy, maybe the ice-pops and hot-dogs aren't doing well, but grass is growing like crazy and your brother's lawn-care business is really strong (at least during the dry hours when he can mow), and because kids love playing in the rain, your sister is probably earning enough from her water park to at least pay you back with that little bit of extra income from the interest payment.

So back to the key question of this section: stocks, bonds or mutual funds?

You can make a fine argument for using mutual funds as the investment of choice when it comes to teaching kids about Wall Street. After all, with one investment your offspring's portfolio is instantly diversified, which erases the risk that a single, soured stock all but wipes out the account. Also, with thousands upon thousands of mutual funds to choose from, you can easily find a fund to fit your specific want, whether a basic Standard & Poor's index fund or something substantially more exotic. Furthermore, mutual funds can be very cost effective since some brokerage firms impose no trading fees for certain mutual funds.

Then again, mutual funds have a glaring weakness when it comes to teaching kids about the stock market: They're boring—and that's a significant flaw when you hope to capture a young investor's attention.

Here's the problem: Mutual funds don't move nearly as dramatically as a stock can. So, for instance, take Google, a name that every kid who has surfed the Internet probably knows well. The company's shares routinely move in relatively big dollar amounts, sometimes $15 or $20 in a day. Inside a mutual fund, the movement of all the other stocks in the portfolio will generally overshadow Google's individual price movement. Indeed, you could well face a situation where the fund itself is down on the day while Google is up. As such, individual shares of stock are a much better choice when it comes to showing kids the interrelation between the stock and an underlying company's business or the economy as a whole.

You can demonstrate this with some mild drama by going online, to sites like Google Finance, Yahoo Finance, CNNMoney. com or even your own brokerage firm's website, and pulling up charts of a company with which a kid is clearly familiar. So let's use the most obvious example, McDonald's, since Ronald and his gang are so widely known among children. First, pull up the day's chart. It will likely show movement of less than a dollar, up or down, probably not a wide span. Next, pull up the charts for the week, the month and the quarter. You and your progeny will see much wider variations in the stock's high and low prices. Finally, pull up charts for one year, five years, ten years, and, if you can, the maximum period available beyond a decade. You will see dramatically wider swings in price. More important—and especially with the longer intervals—you will see a clear upward trend in McDonald's stock price. That's the long-term profits of owning the company as it grows bigger and bigger through the years. In Mickey D's case, the maximum chart period available on Google Finance, a 30-year run, shows the burger chain's near-inexorable rise from just over $1 a share in January 1978 to about $60 by mid-2009.

Mutual funds are best employed in your child's college savings account, which isn't a tool for teaching investment skills but, rather, an account that should be invested prudently for the future. Mutual funds are also the generally preferred option for saving in retirement accounts such as an IRA or a 401(k), which I'll discuss in an upcoming section. In both instances, mutual funds are the appropriate vehicle because they are less risky than individual shares and are professionally managed.

Corporate bonds can also work as a means of teaching kids about investing. So, too, can so-called preferred shares, which act a lot like a hybrid between a stock and a bond. Each has the benefit of being far more stable than stocks, generally speaking, meaning they won't gyrate as wildly as common stocks can. And they spin off regular interest or dividend payments, which kids will like.

Still, a disconnect remains between company news and the

movement in the price of bonds and preferred stocks. Neither shares the characteristics that make common stock so reflective of a company's business operations or the overall economy. Bonds and preferred stock are, instead, more tied to a company's credit worthiness. So assuming a company remains creditworthy in the eyes of those who track such stuff, that company's bonds and preferred stock aren't going to react much to earnings announcements or a new drug approval or whatever—and kids really aren't going to see Wall Street in action.

For that reason, I'm going to focus on stocks as the teaching tool of choice since stocks, much more so than bonds and mutual funds and other types of investments, speak directly to the ways of Wall Street.

Where to Begin
· · · · · · · · · · · · · · · ·

Jump right in: Begin with the definition of a stock in terms that resonates with kids. To do that, let's pick on McDonald's again, since it's such a kid-friendly name. (By the way, before you begin this lesson you might consider first opening the low-commission brokerage account mentioned earlier—if you don't already have a brokerage account. Then buy one share of McDonald's or some other company with which you know your child is intimately familiar, such as Coca-Cola, the Walt Disney Co. or even the local, publicly traded grocery store, like Kroger or Albertsons or Wal-Mart. Ask your broker to send you the physical certificate, which will probably cost you an additional $25 or so. Having a real share of stock that your child can hold and examine will make this lesson sink in.)

Buying a share of stock, a single share of Mickey D's,

means that at the most basic level you own a little piece of the McDonald's down the street. Of course, owning that one share of McDonald's doesn't mean you actually own the store, or that you can bebop through the doors and feed yourself for free. But it does mean that you're entitled to a tiny, tiny sliver of money from every burger and shake and Happy Meal sold there, and that you're entitled to a tiny, tiny sliver of every burger and shake and Happy Meal sold at each of the more than 30,000 McDonald's eateries around the world.

That single Mickey D's share also means McDonald's promises to pay you a little bit of money every year—a dividend payment—as your share of the money the company earned by selling all those burgers and shakes and Happy Meals all over the world. As McDonald's builds more and more restaurants through the years, and as the company earns more and more from all the new restaurants and new types of food it offers, each share of stock can be more and more valuable. It's worth more to other investors, meaning you can sell that share for more money than you originally spent to buy it. So you have two ways to make money: You get those dividends every year, and your stock can go up in value.

The best part is you don't have to do anything but own that share of stock. You can put it in your sock drawer and go to school every day and play on the weekends and take vacations—and the whole time you're doing that, your share of McDonald's is working to earn money for you.

And that's pretty much a stock.

With some kids, that bit of knowledge might prompt a series of questions either in the moment, or that arise over time as your child digests the information. So, let's deal with them in a similar Q&A fashion:

Q: Can we go to McDonald's now and buy a Happy Meal and some stock? (or, Where do you buy stock?)

A: No. You buy stock through a stockbroker. You have to open what is called a brokerage account. You tell the brokerage firm what you want to buy, and you send the money to your account to pay for it. I've already opened an account for you (assuming this is true) so that we can begin investing together when you feel ready. It's online, so you can see the account on the computer, and we can buy stock using the computer.

Q: Does McDonald's pay us to own stock?

A: Yes and no. They don't pay us every week like they pay the people who work at McDonald's. But because we're one of the owners of the company, McDonald's shares with us some of the money it earns from selling all that food to people around the world. It does that by sending us something called a *dividend check* a few times a year. So if we own, say, 100 shares of McDonald's stock, and McDonald's pays 50 cents for every share that people like us own, then we get $50 in the mail. They do this four times a year, so we'll get $200.

Then, there's something called *capital appreciation*, which basically means our shares of McDonald's stock go up in value over time as Mickey D's gets bigger and bigger. So we might buy the stock when each share is $50, and then if we hold it as the company gets bigger it might be worth $75 or $100. So we get "paid" that way, too.

Q: How much does stock cost?

A: That depends on the stock you buy. Some cost just a few pennies or a few dollars a share; some cost a few hundred dollars each. Most, though, are between $10 and about $75.

Q: Can you own more than one share?

A: Yes. You can own as many shares as you can afford. The more shares you own, the bigger your dividend checks, and the more money you make if the shares go up in value.

Q: What would happen if *everyone* stopped eating at McDonald's? (or, Can you lose the money you invested in the stock?)

A: Well, that's the risk of investing. The stock you buy can go down and you can lose money if you sell the shares for less than you bought them for. That's why you want to take time to think about what you want to invest in and research the company. You don't want to invest in some company just because it has stock. Thousands of companies offer stock, but not every company is a good company, and not every stock is a good stock.

Q: Do you have to own stock for a certain amount of time?

A: Nope. You can buy today and sell it one minute later if you wanted to. You could sell it tomorrow or next month. Or you could hold it 20 years or more. It just depends on when you decide you want to sell. But most people who buy stock— they're called *investors*—usually keep the stocks they buy for years. If you think about it, you're buying a piece of a company, and companies take time to grow bigger, just like it takes you time to grow bigger. And that's the point of being an investor: You want your money to grow bigger over time as the company gets bigger over time.

Q: Can we buy stock in other companies besides McDonald's?

A: Sure. We can buy stock in, like, 8,000 companies. I don't even know them all. But there are a lot you would recognize because we shop there, or we eat there, or you buy your video games there, or we've flown on their airplanes or stayed in their hotels. Companies like Home Depot, Albertsons, American Airlines, Hilton Hotels, the Walt Disney Co., Kellogg's (the cereal company that makes your Frosted Flakes), Google and GameStop, the video game store. There's just a ton of these companies that you probably know.

Q: Are all of those good companies to buy?

A: Some yes; some no. We need to look at them together and determine what we like and whether it's a good company we might want to own.

Kid-Friendly Stocks

When you do get around to picking out stocks together, gravitate to those more inclined to fuel your child's interest in investing, and that can help you teach the ways of Wall Street.

First and foremost, stick to companies your child recognizes for one reason or another. A pharmaceutical company such as Pfizer or Merck might well prove to be a fine investment over time, and it might pay a nice dividend (an important benefit in teaching kids about stocks and for keeping them interested in their stocks, and we'll get to that in just a moment), but neither is likely to resonate with a young mind because there's no experiential reference to draw upon.

Certainly, companies like toymaker Hasbro or video game company Nintendo and the Walt Disney Co. are obvious selections, but don't focus singularly on a relatively small collection of clearly kid-centric companies. That's too limiting, and it underestimates a child's interest and economic knowledge base. Kids interact in the economy all the time with Mom and Dad and grandparents, either actively buying something or watching transactions occur. Companies that tend to resonate well with kids are retailers and restaurants, since kids often shop or go to dinner with Mom or Dad and can understand what the company does simply by dint of repeated exposure. And with that, we come to another rule:

Kids & Money Rule #10: When it comes to investing in stocks, kids should understand a company at such a basic level that they can draw a picture of the business model with a crayon.

It's not hard, for instance, to understand what Wal-Mart or McDonald's do to earn money. They sell things. And it's not hard to explain to a child how the company earns more money next year—by selling *more* of those things.

Dividends are the other key criterion. Money arriving in the mail every few months gives kids a tangible benefit of owning stock. Capital appreciation is certainly nice, but it's not routine. A particular stock can go for long stretches with little or no movement. Or shares might fall, never much fun to watch on a monthly basis when the account statements arrive. But dividends bring some life to the learning because they are routine with well-managed companies. Even if the stock does nothing to gain in value, or even if it loses value, the dividend will show your child that the shares still provide financial benefit.

Unless you own the shares directly, the dividend checks won't actually land in your mailbox, but rather in your kid's brokerage account. And while the impact of seeing money accumulate in your account is nice, it doesn't begin to compare to actually receiving a physical check in the mail made out in your name. Those checks drive home the point that investing can increase your wealth. So ask your broker to have the stock certificates registered in your name and delivered to your address (just keep them in a secure spot, like a family safe or a bank safe-deposit box). The dividend checks will follow thereafter. You don't need to have your broker send certificates for every stock you and your child ultimately buy. One or two, maybe three companies in certificate form are enough for your child to experience the excitement of receiving dividend checks and to begin appreciating the benefits of investing. To the degree it's possible based upon your research, try to find companies on different dividend cycles, meaning one pays quarterly dividends on a January, April, July, October cycle, while another pays in February, May, August and November. And assuming you do decide to own three stocks that send dividend checks directly to your house, find a third company that pays on the March, June, September, December cycle—that way your child will receive a dividend check every month.

You can fit that money into your child's overall allowance scheme, however you have that scheme arranged. Or, to teach yet another lesson of investing, you can require that the checks be deposited back into the brokerage account so that the money can be reinvested in additional shares of stock. The lesson: compounding; that is, earning additional money off the money you've already earned.

So start your adventure on Wall Street by making a list of dividend-paying, kid-friendly companies that you and your child can research together. Here's a list of some dividend-paying stocks to consider, and a bit of information about those companies where the name alone might not be enough to jog your memory. (And don't worry if you don't know how to find out if a stock pays a dividend; I'll show you how later in this chapter.) I'm not implying that all of these are buy-list companies, or that these are the only companies to consider, just that they are names kids will probably recognize. Which ones, if any, you should buy depends on your own research. (By the way, the stock market symbols accompanying each company below, and the fact that these companies paid dividends, were accurate as of spring 2009; they could change over time as companies move from one stock exchange to another. Dividends, meanwhile, could be eliminated for various financial reasons. Also, each company was a stock-exchange-listed firm, though that, too, could change as companies are purchased by rivals or go private.)

- McDonald's (symbol: MCD)
- Burger King (BKC)
- Wendy's/Arby's Group (WEN)
- Yum Brands (YUM), operates a host of chains kids know: KFC, Pizza Hut and Taco Bell, among others.
- Walt Disney Co. (DIS)
- Coca-Cola Co. (KO)
- Pepsico (PEP), the company behind Pepsi, Tropicana, Gatorade, Frito-Lay and Quaker Oats
- The Hershey Co. (HSY)
- Tootsie Roll Industries (TR)
- Campbell Soup Co.(CPB)
- Mattel (MAT), America's toy giant
- Hasbro (HAS), another toy behemoth

- Wal-Mart (WMT)
- Home Depot (HD)
- Lowe's (LOW), the other Home Depot
- Kroger (KR), a supermarket chain
- Whole Foods Market (WFMI), a high-end supermarket chain
- Sony (SNE), maker of the PlayStation video game system
- Microsoft (MSFT)
- Nintendo (NTDOY), maker of the Wii and a host of popular video games
- Kellogg's (K), think: Rice Krispies, Eggos, PopTarts and a host of breakfast goodies
- General Mills (GIS), silly Rabbit! This company sells everything from Trix cereal to Progresso soups to Häagen-Dazs ice cream
- Darden Restaurants (DRI), runs the Olive Garden and Red Lobster chains, among others
- Abercrombie & Fitch (ANF), a teen-centric clothing retailer
- The Gap (GPS), another clothing retailer teens are familiar with
- American Eagle Outfitters (AEO), yet another young-consumer clothing purveyor
- World Wrestling Entertainment (WWE)

Of course, not every kid-friendly company pays a dividend. Non-dividend payers are often higher growth companies that are using the money they'd otherwise be paying in dividends to instead make the company bigger and better by investing in research and development or building new stores or buying other companies. These companies, instead of sending out dividend payments, work on the assumption that investors will profit through capital appreciation as the stock price increases over time alongside the company's growth.

So long as you own one or two or three that do pay dividends, then it's fine to own some that don't. Here are several companies that are kid-friendly and that don't pay a dividend (at least not as of 2009) but which you might still consider:

- GameStop (GME), a retailer of video game systems and game disks
- Electronic Arts (ERTS), the maker of such popular video game titles as *Madden NFL* and *Tiger Woods PGA Tour*
- Activision Blizzard (ATVI), another video game maker, this one behind the wildly popular *Guitar Hero, Call of Duty* and *World of Warcraft* franchises
- Build-A-Bear Workshop (BBW)
- Google (GOOG)
- Apple (AAPL)
- Dreamworks Animation SKG (DWA), the moviemakers behind *Shrek, Chicken Run* and *Madagascar,* among other animated movies
- eBay (EBAY)
- Crocs (CROCX), the shoemaker
- Starbucks (SBUX)
- Gymboree (GYMB)
- Sonic (SONC), a drive-in burger chain
- Jack in the Box (JBX), another fast-food empire
- CEC Entertainment (CEC), the Chuck E. Cheese pizza chain

- Tween Brands (TWB), the company running the Limited Too and Justice apparel chains
- Hot Topic (HOTT), a trendy teen-oriented retailer
- Pacific Sunwear of California (PSUN), one more teen retailer
- Krispy Kreme Doughnuts (KKD)
- Marvel Entertainment (MVL), the comic-book giant with characters such as Spider Man, Ironman, X-Men and many more
- Six Flags (SIX), the amusement park company

These lists could go on and on, and you can expand the companies as fits your family's experiences. That means you could include travel companies such as Marriott International (MAR) or Starwood Hotels & Resorts Worldwide (HOT) or Southwest Airlines (LUV). It could include local banks you deal with, such as Bank of America (BAC) or whatever publicly traded neighborhood bank is in your area. Even the local water and electric utilities make the list, since your kids will likely be familiar with them in some fashion.

Research Before You Buy

This is the fun part. This is where you get to spend time with your kid "kicking the tires," in Wall Street's jargon. As you'll see, this is why it makes sense to stick with companies and concepts your child is already familiar with. It will make the research that much more enjoyable and, thus, more likely to resonate.

Skipping to the end for a moment, the ultimate message

you're trying to send is that a) research isn't nearly as complex as you might imagine, and b) success as an investor comes from your own analysis, not believing singularly in the musings of others who purport to be experts.

At a kid level, research consists of checking out the companies you're both interested in (physically, if possible) and spending some time examining a company's *investor relations* page on its website.

Where possible, pay a visit to a company's stores. Many of the companies on the previous lists are national retailers or restaurants, and chances are pretty good that some operate a business you can physically inspect in your area. Spend time in the stores on several occasions and note the number of cars that are, or are not, in the parking lot (though this won't work for mall-based retailers such as Build-A-Bear Workshops or Abercrombie & Fitch). Are the stores clean? Are many shoppers strolling the aisles? Do shelves look disheveled or well-stocked? Is inventory lying around in boxes? With clothes retailers, do the fashions on display match the fashions you see most kids wearing, or do they look too trendy or too dated? If it's a store or restaurant your family often visits, does it seem like more or fewer customers are there? Has the quality changed for better or worse?

True, these are basic, simple observations. But simple can be very powerful. Numbers can certainly tell you a more complete story at some point, but these gut reactions can tell you long before the numbers are released whether some company is headed in the right or wrong direction. So, bring a notepad on your research outing and let your child make notes of the observations you both make. Ask probing questions designed to get your little investor thinking about the implications of what you see. If the lines are longer than normal at McDonald's, ask your child what that might say about the chain's popularity and how all those extra people eating at Mickey D's might show up in the money the company earns.

At the core, that's what basic stock analysis really is— observing how well a company is doing.

Of course, you can't really judge that in person with some firms, like, say, Google or Hershey or Nintendo. But there are other ways of getting at that through the company's investor relations website, where you'll find quarterly and annual financial reports, details of the company's businesses, and often presentation slides that executives give to professional investors at investor conferences—all of which you can download in just a few minutes. Or, for a more hands-on approach, contact the company's investor relations department and ask to receive the most recent two or three years of annual and quarterly reports so that you and your child can examine the reports together.

Don't be intimidated by the reports. Though they're filled with what can be esoteric and mind-numbing minutiae, they can be interesting reading at times, particularly the annual reports. Companies typically go all out on them—often through glossy, picture-laden booklets—in order to put on a great face for their investors. Certainly you should learn to read these reports with a jaundiced eye, since companies have every reason to be overly boosterish. Nevertheless, annual reports are a great source of information on everything a company builds or sells, and generally they include annual letters from the chairman and other corporate executives that recap the previous year and look ahead to the coming year. These letters are generally written in plain English, making them clear and concise. As such, they can be highly beneficial in understanding the issues, challenges and opportunities a company faces from the perspective of the people running the place.

Many parts of the report you might not care about, particularly all the footnotes that chronicle a bunch of inside-baseball statistics and financial movements, and that's fine. Again, you're not trying to grow your own mini-MBA. You don't have to consume every last bit of an annual report, and clearly kids aren't going to be interested in any of that anyway. Nevertheless, you and your child can pull out some basic financial observations that are key to the success of any business:

- Are sales, the proverbial "top line," going up or down? If sales volume isn't headed higher over time, then what's the point?

- Are profits, the proverbial "bottom line," going up or down? Stocks are routinely valued based upon how much money the company earns, the annual net profits after all the bills and taxes and such are paid. As such, you want to see profits moving progressively higher, so that the stock price moves progressively higher.

- Does the company pay a dividend and, if so, has the payout been increasing over time? Companies that consistently pay a dividend, and that have routinely raised the amount over time, are often solid, stable companies, though that's not universally true. Dividends can be a useful indicator of strength because while accounting rules allow companies to play all sorts of magical games with the financials they report, a dividend in hand is hard to fake. It's a sign generally that some level of profit is authentic.

- Is the number of stores growing (assuming it's a retailer)? Growth is good as it's a sign a company's concept is taking root outside its original market, which means it has a larger customer base to tap into.
- Is the company expanding into new regions or countries, or getting its products into more stores, or, in the case of Internet companies, attracting more visitors to its websites? Is it creating new and better products that its key consumers want? McDonald's has fairly well reached as many corners of Main Street USA as it can. But there are plenty of Main Streets in China, Brazil, Russia and elsewhere for the company to exploit—even a company as large as McDonald's.
- What is management saying between the lines in its letter to shareholders? You'll probably need to help decipher this since kids haven't lived long enough to grasp the nuances that might be present in the letter. But you can tell if there is an underlying upbeat or downbeat tone to the letter, an optimistic or worrisome air. That will help guide you when considering the important numbers mentioned in the bullet points above.

Certainly, many other observations and data points go into a full-blown, professional analysis of a stock, but that's sort of not your aim here. You're not trying to turn a few dollars your child receives as a holiday gift into an overnight fortune that will fund college and a first house. Your only goal is to introduce your budding investor to the ways of Wall Street, and that's limited to knowing, first, how to spend some time researching the basics of what the company does in order to get a better feel for whether you think the business makes sense and, later, how to buy stocks.

Over time, if your child grows increasingly interested in the stock market, a number of excellent books exist to help flesh out the more detailed due diligence that investors undertake before investing. And if you get to that point, well, that just means you did a great job on the basics of this chapter in helping foster that interest at a young age.

NUMBERS TO KNOW

While professional investors rely on numerous financial ratios to gauge the worthiness and value of individual stocks, there are only two you need to familiarize your children with: the price-earnings ratio and the dividend yield.

Neither number is crucial for a child to master in order to understand investing at a pre-college age. I offer this as a sidebar only because you will come across these terms when investing, and you might want to incorporate them into your lessons when your offspring is old enough to understand the concepts or care about them. If your child never cares, no worries; you will have done the most important work simply in teaching her about investing to begin with.

The P/E ratio, as it's widely known, essentially measures how expensive or cheap a stock currently is relative to the amount of money it earns in a given year. The math is simple: price (P) divided by earnings (E). That's it. So a $30 stock of a company that earns $3 a share in some year trades a P/E of 10.

And what does this P/E ratio tell you? By itself, not much. A P/E of 10 could be high or low depending on the company itself, the industry it's in, and the state of the overall stock market. Historically, the stock market has traded at a P/E in mid-teens. Anything below that and the market is generally considered cheap; above that and the market is generally expensive.

You can apply that to the company itself. If a stock has historically traded in a P/E range of, say, 13 to 17, then a P/E of 10 might be cheap. By contrast, if the stock typically trades around seven, then 10 could be expensive. Thus, the trick with the P/E ratio is to compare the current P/E with historical numbers to get a feel for how the stock is priced relative to its own history. You can find historical P/E ratios for free at Morningstar.com. Click on the "10-Yr Valuation" tab under the "Valuation Ratios" link.

The dividend yield is just as easy to calculate and also serves as a valuation measure. Calculate yield by dividing the annual dividend payment by the current price. So, if a company pays $1 a share in dividends this year and the stock is traded at $30, its yield is 3.3%.

Just like the P/E, yield can serve as a measure of current value, not just a measure of how much money you're earning annually by holding the stock. As the price of a stock goes up, its yield gets smaller; as the price falls, the yield rises. For those who learn visually, it looks like this:

If that $30 stock rises to $50 and the dividend remains at $1 a share, the yield drops to 2%. If the stock falls to $15, the yield rises to 6.7%.

As such, when a stock's yield is sharply higher than its historical norms, the shares are likely priced expensively. Likewise, when the yield is sharply lower than normal, that can denote shares that are cheap. Of course, there are exceptions. A very high yield could be a sign of a troubled company, since investors will drive down the share price amid worries about a company's financial future long before the problems require the company to cut its dividend payments to conserve cash. Thus, yield can be a good indicator of value as well as a warning sign.

Again, these numbers border on the mind-numbing and geeky, I know. If you want to do some homework together in researching the valuation of a stock you might be interested in, these are good starting points. If not, no sweat.

DRiP DRiP DRiP: Dividend Reinvestment Plans

Numerous companies offer a plan in which dividends are automatically reinvested in additional, fractional shares of company stock. These so-called DRiP plans can be a very good way to help your kids build a bit of wealth almost absentmindedly, since the only exertion required is that you sign up your child for the program. After that, all the dividends paid by the com-

pany will automatically roll into more and more shares. Over
the years, that can add up to a significant sum.

> **Kids & Money Rule #11:** You don't need to be wealthy to begin
> teaching your children about the stock market.

What makes DRiPs so appealing for teaching kids about
investing is that the plans are so easy on a parent's pocketbook.
You often pay no fees or transaction costs, as you would when
buying shares through a broker. And more than 1,100 companies offer a DRiP requiring a minimum initial purchase of just
one share. That means for an outlay of less than $31 (in mid-
2009), you can get your child into a single share of Campbell
Soup Co., a name just about any kid would likely recognize.

Many companies, once you own one or more shares, often
allow DRiP investors to send in additional dollars every month
or every quarter to buy additional fractional shares. And, just
to sweeten the pot slightly more, some companies reinvest
participants' money at a slight discount to the stock's current
market price. In terms of your ongoing efforts at educating your
youngster, you can work these benefits into your overall saving
and investing strategies by, for instance, encouraging your
child to direct part of his savings into additional purchases of
the stock.

DRiP programs keep the shares in your name (or your
child's name, as the case may be) and the companies typically
dispatch a quarterly account statement detailing all the activity: how much money was earned in dividends and how many
additional shares those dividends bought; how many shares

your child purchased with the additional money, if any, that was sent in; and how many total shares exist in the account. By incorporating those statements into your financial lessons, you can demonstrate to your child that even when he's not paying attention, when he's out playing soccer or riding a bike or going to school or sleeping or watching TV, his money is at work generating even more money.

Check with the companies you seek to own to determine if they offer a DRiP; many will spell it out on their investor-relations page on their website. Or, check out a website like www.directinvesting.com, which is home to all things DRiP. The site charges a fee for most of its services; however, you can peruse the "Search for DRIPs" link to at least determine which companies offer the program.

The downside to DRiPs is that each company runs its own plan, so if you sign up for several DRiPs you could end up with a good deal of paperwork to keep track of—and you will need that paperwork whenever you sell the shares to document your cost basis, or the total cost of all the shares you sold.

From an educational viewpoint, DRiPs are best instituted only after your child has experienced the excitement of receiving a dividend check in the mail for a year or so, after the excitement has worn off and it becomes a bit routine. The main purpose of seeking out dividend-paying stocks in the first place is to engage your kids in the investment process, the idea being that regularly receiving a check in the mail will help drive home some of the benefits of calling yourself an investor. If you rush into a DRiP, you lose some of that—though if the low-cost economics of a DRiP work best for your family, then certainly pursue it. With a DRiP you'll still see the dividends arrive on the account statement and accumulate in the form of more and more shares of stock, but, as noted before, a physical check made out in a kid's name will engrain the message more deeply than will an account statement.

Retirement Savings—for Kids

Let's see: In the choice between spending money on clothes or an iPod, or stashing that money in an account you can't touch until you're almost 60 years old, teens will naturally scoff at the old-age savings account. Sixty? Geez, that's like dog's years from now—at least to a teen. The iPod is necessary for *today.*

Nevertheless, saving for retirement is an increasingly important skill, given the death of company pension plans and many, many questions about the viability of the Social Security system as we know it. Today's parents and grandparents will benefit from Social Security, but our kids and grandkids might not be as lucky, or, assuming the system survives in some fashion, may receive limited benefits. Worse, medical advances mean today's youth have a very good chance of living to 100 and beyond. They're going to need a bundle of cash to help pay their costs.

As such, learning to save for retirement is a primary message all parents should instill in their offspring. You have a few ways to do this, including Individual Retirement Accounts (IRAs) and 401(k) plans for teens who work, and variable annuities for younger kids who aren't old enough to join the workforce. No doubt that teaching a child to save some part of every paycheck for retirement is a hard sell. Retirement to a teenager is so far from reality that seeing Scooby Doo walking down the street seems more likely. Most kids really aren't going to want to give up a portion of their pay for an event so far in the future because that pay is usually fairly limited to begin with. Instead, they want to use that money to satisfy so many other pressing financial needs: gas for the car, cash for iTunes downloads, their cell phone bills, new clothes, dating—their list is as endless as yours.

But there are ways to incentivize a youngster, mainly by offering to rebate all or a portion of the money your child saves in an IRA or 401(k). A rebate sends the message that you deeply believe retirement savings is *that* important (and the message will sink in), and it helps to develop a savings ethic that will roll over into your child's first job after college. That's where saving for retirement will really mean something, because study after study has demonstrated that those who begin saving the earliest have a far easier road to retirement and far fewer financial worries once they're there. Through compounding, those early dollars, though small in number, work the hardest over many, many years, making it much easier to reach the ultimate goal.

IRAs for Kids

Let me say at the outset that there's no such creature as a kid-specific IRA. Nevertheless, kids are free to open and fund a traditional or Roth IRA once they earn income that is reportable to the IRS. That generally means teenagers, once they're working in their first job, are eligible to begin saving in a tax-advantaged retirement account.

Teens can contribute up to the maximum IRA contribution for the year ($5,000 in 2009), or, if they earn less than the maximum, they can donate their entire earned income. Put another way, if a teen earns, say, $3,500 working as a lifeguard over the summer, she can contribute $3,500 to an IRA. If she earns $7,000, she can contribute just $5,000 (at least in 2009; that number will generally change every year, based on inflation, starting in 2010).

The process of opening and funding the account is generally the same as the one I mentioned earlier in this chapter for a standard brokerage account. In all likelihood, you can open an IRA in your child's name with the same brokerage firm.

Though both traditional and Roth IRA options are available, the Roth is clearly the path you want to push your child toward. The key difference between the two types of IRAs centers on how each is treated in tax terms.

With a traditional IRA you get:

- **A tax deduction up front,** meaning your teen's annual IRA contribution reduces the amount of taxable income reported to the IRS, lowering the tax bill;
- **Tax-deferred growth until the money is withdrawn at retirement,** meaning all of your teen's contribution is at work and she'll pay no taxes on profits, interest and dividends while the money is in the account;
- **Full tax treatment upon withdrawal,** meaning the full amount of each withdrawal is taxed as ordinary income at whatever tax rates exist at that time;
- **Limitations on accessing the money in the account until age 59½,** meaning the government imposes taxes on the full amount of the cash withdrawn, plus an additional penalty of 10% of the amount withdrawn, if it is withdrawn before the child turns 59½.

With a Roth IRA you get:

- **No tax deduction each year,** meaning your teen's contribution comes from after-tax dollars. The upshot there is that your teen is taking a bigger bite out of her income to afford the same level of contribution (after all, if she's in the 10% tax bracket, she must earn $3,889 as a lifeguard to afford that $3,500 contribution after paying the taxes she'll owe);

- **Tax-deferred growth,** meaning, like with the traditional IRA, no taxes are due on profits, interest and dividends while the money is in the account;

- **Tax-free withdrawals at retirement,** meaning your teen, once she's retired, owes no taxes whatsoever on any of the money. This is a huge benefit, as I'll explain shortly.

- **Greater flexibility for accessing the money,** meaning that so long as your teen has owned the account for more than five years, she can withdraw, prior to age 59½, all the principal she has invested without paying taxes or penalties. Withdrawing the earnings early, however, would incur the same taxes and penalties associated with a traditional IRA.

The clear choice for teens is the Roth IRA because of the tax-free advantages it provides in retirement. Here's why: Teens rarely earn enough in their part-time jobs to pay big taxes, thus the small tax bite imposed on their income is insignificant, at best. In retirement, however, after decades of saving, your grown child's income could be substantial enough to push her into the higher, if not the highest tax brackets, where the tax bite is substantially more painful. With the Roth, you trade an

insignificant tax break as a teenager for a potentially monu-
mental tax break as a retiree.

Think about it in real dollar terms for a moment. Save in a
traditional IRA as a teen, and that $3,500 contribution saves
all of $350 in taxes—probably meaningful when you're 16, but
imperceptible in the grand scheme. After 51 years of saving
$3,500 annually in a Roth (saving from age 16 to retirement at
67), the account value would exceed $1.5 million (assuming a
fairly mundane 7% yearly return). Pull just 4% of that sum out
of a traditional IRA in the first year to live on and you're paying
taxes of more than $15,000 to the IRS, assuming a middle-of-
the road tax rate of 25%. A similar tax obligation accrues each
and every year.

With the Roth, your teen would have effectively paid taxes
every year on the contributions since they're after-tax dollars
going in. Depending on what tax rate your teen falls into each
year, the total taxes paid over the decades could range between
$20,000 to $50,000. But, since Roths impose no tax burden,
after just three or four years of withdrawals your child is ahead
of the game—and every penny after that is truly tax free. Moreover, because of the Roth's tax advantages, the value of the
nest egg goes so much further in retirement. If, for instance,
your child needs $75,000 a year to live on in her golden years,
a Roth only requires a distribution of $75,000. A traditional
IRA would require a withdrawal of $100,000—assuming that
25% tax bracket—to meet the same $75,000 need after taxes
are deducted. That depletes the account more rapidly.

So while skipping the tax benefit today might be somewhat
detrimental to your teen's wealth near term, she's sure to be
grateful in retirement that you had the foresight and wisdom to
steer her to a Roth in her first job.

And as for where your teenage worker should invest her

IRA contributions, be simple about it—just guide her toward a plain-vanilla, low-cost S&P 500 stock-index fund, like those offered by Vanguard (the Vanguard 500 Index Fund) or Fidelity (the Fidelity Spartan 500 Index Fund). They're about as inexpensive as you'll find—Fidelity charges just 1/10 of 1% annually, or $1 for every $1,000 invested—and your child will benefit from the overall growth of the U.S. economy. If you're concerned about broader diversity, suggest your teen stuff 20% to 30% of the money in an international-stock index fund. Overseas markets, simply because of their size relative to the U.S. market and their exploding mass of middle-class consumers, offer the prospect of faster economic growth over the years. And because your teen has so many decades before touching the money, exposure to faster-growing companies in faster-growing markets will likely prove beneficial.

401(K)ids Account

Along with IRAs goes the 401(k) as a popular and nearly ubiquitous retirement-savings account. The big problem when it comes to teenage workers, however, is that they're often shut out.

The jobs teens gravitate toward, such as flipping burgers, selling clothes at teen-centric retailers in the mall, or working the supermarket cash register, usually don't offer any type of retirement-savings benefits because employers have the ability to exclude certain workers from the plan based on age or number of hours worked. In many cases that means anyone under 18 or 21 can't contribute to the company's 401(k) plan, nor can those who work less than 1,000 hours a year, which is roughly 19.2 hours a week.

But nothing is stopping you from making your own plan—what I call the "401(K)ids Account."

Just to be clear, this is not a *real* retirement-savings plan. There is no such thing, so no need to call Charles Schwab or Merrill Lynch asking how to open one. Rather, this is a fictitious plan I made up to teach my own young son about the stock market and to encourage him to think about investing his money instead of spending it on yet another video game.

The concept steals liberally from the 401(k) plans found all over corporate America.

For those unfamiliar with how a 401(k) works, it is similar to a traditional IRA in that you earn a tax break on the dollars you contribute to the plan each year; your money then grows tax-deferred until retirement, at which point you pay taxes when you begin withdrawing it. The key difference is that an employer generally contributes a bit of money to the account too, often 25 cents to 50 cents for every dollar a worker contributes. So, contribute $100 from a paycheck and, at 50 cents to the dollar, the account will show a balance of $150. And that's before any money is ever invested. Not bad; a 50% return on your money for simply contributing to the account. Basically, free money—the best kind of money.

Since your young worker likely won't be allowed to enroll in a 401(k) plan while working part-time, you'll have to create your own 401(K)ids plan. The aim isn't so much to accumulate a bunch of money as it is to teach your child about the necessity of saving for retirement. You're also aiming to acclimate them to the idea of forsaking part of their earnings, and to show them through that process that giving up a small piece of your paycheck can be relatively painless.

The plan is very simple:

For every dollar that your child saves and puts to work in

the stock market, offer to match it one for one. That's it. I told
you it was simple. You can adjust the match to fit your family's
means, but you should try to keep your contribution meaningful enough to capture your child's interest, so you should top up
their contribution by at least 50%.

You can use this plan for working teens or younger children
who are at least 12 years old or so. With working teens you'll
be matching whatever portion of their paycheck they agree to
put aside and invest. Establish the amount with your child,
and don't let him alter it every week to meet whatever spending needs emerge. Your young worker's contribution needs to
remain static so that it becomes a routine payment (and that's
what a 401(k) contribution really is—a payment on your future
costs).

Nonworking younger kids generally don't have regular
income, although an allowance fits that description to some
degree. With these youngsters, pledge to match whatever portion of the birthday/holiday money they receive and opt to
invest in the 401(K)ids plan. With allowances, agree to offer up
a matching contribution if your child agrees to invest a certain
percentage of the money in her Spending jar at the end of every
month. Again, keep the amount static; you're aiming to teach
discipline and consistency. And you want the money coming
from the Spending jar rather than the Savings jar because a
traditional 401(k) plan is based on contributions pulled from a
paycheck, which, for all practical purposes, limits discretionary
spending. Might as well get a child accustomed to that now.

What you really want to emphasize when detailing your
plan is that you're talking about free money. You're willing to
give them $1 (or 50 cents, as the case may be) for every dollar
saved. And the money is theirs to keep forever; you will never

take it back. Encourage them to save until it hurts, though kids might not necessarily agree to that. Still, saving anything will instill the lessons you want them to learn about 401(k) plans.

In complementing your broader lessons on investing, consider incorporating a 401(K)ids account into your stock-market teachings. Use that standard brokerage account you and your child open as the 401(K)ids account.

As with the IRA mentioned previously, you can simplify the investment component of a 401(K)ids account by steering a youngster's cash into a basic, low-cost S&P index fund such as the ones noted earlier. Personally, I'd encourage you to specifically not match money dumped into a savings account. That's for the money from the Savings jar. With the 401(K)ids account, you want your child to become comfortable with stocks and investing, since that's where the best returns will largely come from over time, the 2008 stock market crash not withstanding.

You will, of course, need an exit strategy as well—the "retirement" date when your child can finally tap into the fund. Two choices: You can disburse the money in a lump sum when college arrives, a strategy that will provide your child with a meaningful bankroll to spend on discretionary wants (or textbooks and the like); or you can distribute the money after college, giving the sum an additional few years to fatten, potentially providing your college grad a nice windfall to help secure their first apartment; to serve as a down payment on a house or car; or to use for a vacation or other spending desires. Indeed, you can keep the 401(K)ids plan operational all through college, if your child decides to work while earning a degree.

Kids and Annuities
. . . .

Annuities are largely thought of as investment products designed for older workers saving for retirement or retirees looking for a stream of income they can never outgrow. However,
annuities can be a fantastic, if unconventional way for parents
or grandparents to invest for a child's long-range future.

An annuity isn't an account you should use to teach your
kids about money, but rather a forward-thinking gift you give to
your kids or grandkids that they will quietly thank you for many,
many years from now when you might not even be around.

An annuity is simply an insurance contract mixed with an
investment component that grows larger over time and that,
when your child reaches retirement, can be annuitized. To annuitize simply means to turn a sum of money into a stream
of monthly income that can be structured to last for a certain
number of years or until death. That means an annuity ultimately can grow from the moment your child or grandchild is
born and then provide income from the moment he or she re-
tires until death—truly a gift that lasts a lifetime.

While there are a variety of annuities, the one you want to
concentrate on for kids is a so-called variable annuity. These
are essentially mutual fund–like investment accounts wrapped
in an insurance contract. The investment account grows over
time based on the performance of the underlying investment,
such as, say, an S&P 500 fund, while the insurance component
offers certain guarantees as well as the ability to annuitize the
contract at some point in retirement.

VAs, as they're called, do not require proof of earned income,
as do IRAs. That means farsighted parents and grandparents

with cash to spare can fund a VA in a child's name. (Most low-cost annuity providers typically require a minimum initial investment of $5,000.) The benefit: The money grows tax-deferred for many decades before the child ever taps into it (taxes are paid at distribution at whatever the child's ordinary tax rate is in retirement). Think about this for moment because it's a rather stunning result: Invest $5,000 on a child's first birthday, never invest another nickel, earn a fairly modest 7% rate of return until the child is 70 years old, and the nest egg is worth more than $532,000. Manage to earn an annual return just a single percentage point higher—8%—and the nest egg exceeds $1 million. That's a heck of gift to hand over. Though it might not fund a full retirement, it will clearly add a nice sweetener to what your child is able to accumulate through years of working and saving.

To be sure, variable annuities have a dark side, and rightly so. Too many annuity peddlers use scare tactics to convince elderly investors that a VA is appropriate and wise. Federal and state regulators have repeatedly censured these sellers and warned buyers away. In short, VAs are largely inappropriate for people already in retirement. But they are wonderful investments for those who still have many years to go, and kids clearly fit that definition.

To make the most of your money, open an annuity account in your child's name in a low-cost variable annuity with a company like Fidelity, Vanguard, TIAA-CREF or Charles Schwab.

Kids and Taxes

Just to round out what you need to know about kids and investing, your child might be subject to taxes, based on the

dividends, interest and capital gains and losses accumulated in
savings and investment accounts. This means your child might
need to file a tax return.

In many cases, kids won't have to file returns if their earnings are less than a certain amount (and that amount changes
over time). Yet filing a return can still be smart because
1) your child can recoup some of the federal taxes during the
year, even if it is a small amount; and 2) reporting the income
makes your child eligible for an IRA contribution. By the same
measure, some counties and cities across the country don't
make taxpayers under 18 pay local taxes, yet those taxes will
likely have been deducted from your child's paycheck during
the year. So filing an individual state return would generate a
refund of those taxes paid.

Depending on the amount of money a child earns, he or she
might be subject to the so-called "kiddie tax," which is generally in the 10% range. But kids who earn more than the "kiddie
tax" limit pay taxes at the parents' tax rate, which can mean a
meaningfully larger bite by local and federal tax agencies. This
book isn't offering any advice on these tax matters, so how all
of this plays out in your child's tax life and yours is best ad-
dressed by an accountant or qualified tax preparer who fully
understands the impact of taxes on kids and their earnings.

Whatever the case, remember this: For the most part, investment decisions should not be made solely because of tax
issues. After all, it's always better to be taxed more heavily on a
large amount of income than to be taxed lightly on a small sum.
Your child will still end up with a fatter wallet.

6

Giving

A CHARITABLE HEART STARTS YOUNG

Birthday parties were once about a pile of presents that kids ripped through almost mindlessly, indifferent to the identity of the gift giver and often forgetting within days the gifts they received. In recent years, though, a more compassionate, sometimes poignant trend has emerged in which kids celebrate their birthdays by tossing aside tradition for a more selfless act: Rather than expecting that pile of presents, a new generation of children and parents are dispatching invites to friends specifically requesting *no presents* at all. Instead, they ask that partygoers arrive with a donation to a particular charitable cause, be it the local children's hospital, an animal shelter or a needy schoolmate's family.

Charity has never gone out of style, of course, but nowadays kids are bringing a style of their own. In large measure it's a style that stems from modern technology. Where child-friendly charity was once comprised mainly of dropping a dollar into a church collection basket or soliciting pocket change for a

March of Dimes drive, the Internet has opened a vast array of possibilities to young givers. The Web delivers pictures, video and stories of pain, loss, hunger and devastation from forgotten wars and natural disasters that are largely sanitized or overlooked by television. That, in turn, is giving kids far greater motivation and many more opportunities to participate in countless outreach efforts that are tied to a wide selection of national and international charitable organizations—many of which aren't likely to have some physical representation in your hometown. Accordingly, charity has turned into something that often comes off as trendy or hip among youngsters who, because of the *cool* factor, want to be part of something larger.

But before your son starts collecting money for a local orphanage, or before your daughter decides she wants to help refugee children in sub-Saharan Africa, they first must be exposed to charity in its various forms and understand why helping those in need is incumbent upon those of means. Without those lessons from Mom and Dad, kids don't know to help.

More important, with those lessons kids learn to help for the rest of their lives. Among other findings, a survey by Independent Sector and Youth Service America found that:

- Two-thirds of adults who volunteer began their charitable activities when they were young;
- Those who volunteer when they're young are twice as likely to volunteer as adults than those who didn't volunteer in their youth;
- In every income range and age group, those who volunteered as youths give more and volunteer more than those who did not volunteer in their early years;
- And those who volunteered when they were young,

and whose parents volunteered, became the most generous adults in terms of their time.

At its core, generosity comes from the heart, not Mom and Dad's lectures on tithing and requirements that youngsters contribute a third of their allowance to the Giving jar. You can babble words all you like, and mandate your child give away every penny, but until your child sees your words in action, all the sentences you string together about donating to the needs of others will ring hollow. For that reason, charity introduces a unique set of financial issues for parents to address, starting when their kids are young. Indeed, young children in particular aren't likely to know the word *philanthropy*, and in their linear way of thinking they have trouble conceptualizing the notion of *need*. If kids haven't experienced desperate times in their own family's situation (and I'm assuming here that most of this book's readers probably aren't coming from war zones or refugee situations or homeless shelters), expecting them to know what it means to be hungry or to wonder where the family will sleep tonight is unrealistic.

Kids connect with what they experience, what they know, and what they see. That could be a relative who suffers from a particular disease, or maybe a classmate whose family lost their home in a fire or flood, and the resulting actions of parents to salve some of the hurt or to advance ongoing efforts to prevent such pain in the future. For Mom and Dad, then, these are life's *teachable moments*—those opportunities that arise during the course of any average day when you can begin explaining what it means to be charitable and why people give their money and their time to help others in need. And that's as good a place as any to start teaching kids about charity.

Teachable Moments
. . . .

Not much benefit is gained by requiring young children to give away part of their money before they really understand the motivation for doing so. Kids don't have many opportunities to earn money and giving away what little they have can be confusing, tormenting or frustrating. And while the "Because I said so" argument works well in many situations as a parent, this really isn't one of those times when forcing your child to abide by your wishes, simply because they're your wishes, teaches the lessons you want them to learn. You want your child to buy into the process of charitable giving, not kowtow to it.

Thus, the teachable moment.

These are the first lessons of charity, and they don't involve your child donating any money. Instead, they represent opportunities for you to show what *need* looks like, to demonstrate the various ways to address it, and, preferably, to show how *you* address it.

Young kids are naturally inquisitive creatures and will often beat you to the punch, asking questions about a given situation while you're still trying to figure out how best to talk about it. So, for instance, if you have a family friend who has a child with special needs, there's a very good chance your child will ask—perhaps indelicately—about the differences he notices in the other child before you get around to it. To the degree you're familiar with the situation, explain the illness or malady responsible for the problem, and how that problem impacts that child's daily life. As well, explain how other people—people like you and your own family—can provide necessary help by donating money, goods or time to efforts aimed at treating the affliction, finding a cure for it or providing services that aid families struggling with the repercussions.

That's philanthropy in a kid-friendly nutshell—helping others who often can't help themselves. Children as young as about six or seven years are capable of understanding that people need help, and they're clearly able to understand the notion of sharing; it's been a prime message of preschool, kindergarten and, likely, life at home. Whether you're talking about animals or the environment, charity at its most fundamental level is about sharing part of what you have with someone else—or some*thing* else. Children can grasp that.

But in keeping with the idea that actions are more important, you need to go beyond the words. You need to demonstrate the ways in which you're personally charitable, either through the money you give or the time you donate to a cause you deem worthy. Begin with a dinner-table conversation in which you explain that you donate time and/or money to a particular cause and why you've made that decision. Make this a show-and-tell exercise; do your research and bring to the table the brochures, pamphlets, photos, props or statistics that illustrate your point. Here's an example taken from www.charitywater.org, a non-profit organization aiming to bring clean drinking water to 1.1 billion (yes, *billion*) people around the world.

Go visit the Charitywater site, and print off some of those pictures of young children collecting muddy water in gasoline cans. Then, bring to the dinner table those photos and the statistic that 42,000 people die every week from a lack of clean water—90% of them kids under the age of five. The pictures and the data will resonate with young minds, which are naturally empathetic.

Once you've established why you give, show your charitable

heart in action. If you donate your time serving food at a soup kitchen, gathering clothes for a women's shelter, or mentoring underprivileged kids at an inner-city school, bring your child along one day to experience what you experience and explain why giving of yourself is so important to who you are.

If you donate money, invite your child into the process. Work together to research online the organizations that serve the need you support. Ask your child if there's a local cause he'd like to support—maybe a local farm that takes in racing greyhounds that have been retired, or the Special Olympics, or even just the local library that needs used books—and brainstorm together how the family might step up to help. Perhaps you could raise money among friends and family or collect goods that can be donated to the cause. Clearly, your child probably won't know about that local farm that cares for retired greyhounds or even that libraries need used books. You'll have to be that fount of knowledge, highlighting causes with which you think your child might potentially connect.

When you and your child find the right charity to support, put your plan into action, either donating some money together or donating some time together.

If nothing else, dedicate a weekend to collecting the unneeded/unused items in your house—as a family—and donate them to organizations that provide clothing and household goods to needy families. This works particularly well with younger children who can collect the toys they no longer play with and then donate them to a children's hospital or a local shelter.

These are small efforts, but they mark the first steps toward a life of caring about the welfare of others.

How Much Is Enough?

Charity is on some level all about money management. After all, you can't be a philanthropist if you spend all your money on toys and clothes and electronics. As such, teaching kids to be philanthropic with their money means teaching them to manage their money with an eye toward setting aside some of their cash to help others.

Back in Chapter 3, I wrote about the Four-Jar Budget and suggested that, once you reach the point where you want your child to start donating some of her own money to charitable causes, you should have her allocate 10% to 15% of her income to philanthropy. That's a good place to start, to get your kids at least thinking and acting in a charitable manner. If nothing else, it generally fits the broad mandates of the world's major religions. Both Christianity and Judaism require adherents to tithe 10% of their income. Followers of Islam, meanwhile, are required to tithe 2.5% of the value of their wealth and possessions. But there's no universal formula here. How much your kid ultimately contributes to charity is a matter of your family's values.

The guidance I'd offer is the same I noted early in the book: You want to set realistic expectations. You can preach to your children that they must contribute one-third of their allowance to the Giving jar, but if you and your spouse don't contribute one-third of your own income to charity, forcing that on a child doesn't make a ton of sense, since one day your child is bound to ask how much you contribute. You can lie and say the amount you donate is bigger than it really is (and that's not such a great way to communicate with your children) or you tell the truth— but then you're stuck explaining a double standard.

So be realistic. And take a cue from your kids in shaping their philanthropic educations. Some children will be enthusiastic about giving and will be more open to allocating a larger portion of their allowance to their Giving jar. Encourage the bourgeoning desire to give. Others will initially be more reticent. Ease them into the process a little slower.

Remember also that you have many other financial lessons—spending, saving, budgeting, investing—that you must teach to your children. As such, you don't want your kids giving away so much that they don't have enough remaining to make the other lessons useful.

Additionally, as I also mentioned initially in Chapter 3, you don't want to create a situation where your child discounts the money being donated, or the allowance you pay, or both. What I mean is this: If you pay your youngster an allowance of $5 a week, but mandate that $2 must go to charity, then your child is just as likely to acknowledge mentally that the *real* allowance is but $3. That other $2 exists only in name, since your child has absolutely no say over the dispensation of those dollars. Your child, in effect, learns not to look at the donation as charity coming from her heart, but as Mom and Dad's money simply passing through her hands. Your child is sacrificing nothing of her own and so your lesson loses its punch.

The Family-Charity Ritual

If you don't yet donate time or money yourself, consider starting a family-charity ritual in which everyone in the family joins in to support a charity the family chooses. Clearly, the end-of-year holidays are an obvious time to hold a family-charity ritual.

The need is widely apparent, philanthropy is in the air, and numerous local organizations provide all manner of support services aimed at helping those in need.

The family, for instance, can play Santa to a poverty-trapped child who has never experienced the wide-eyed joy of a Christmas morning laden with multiple presents under the tree. Suggest that your child 1) pick a wish off a local "angel tree" at the mall; 2) go buy the gift with his own money; and 3) deliver the gift to the charity that distributes the presents to the needy children. Instead of spending Thanksgiving eating turkey and flopping on the couch for a football game, donate several hours as a family to a soup kitchen to display compassion for people and families with less means.

But don't let the family-charity ritual rise up once a year around a major holiday and then die. Needs exist 365 days a year, offering a multitude of opportunities to work with your child to provide services or donations in your community.

To effect that goal, consider creating a *family-charity fund* in which you and your children—and possibly even grandparents, aunts, uncles—all contribute money that you tap into during the year to support a particular cause, or even multiple causes.

Don't assume you can't launch your own family-charity fund because you're not wealthy. Philanthropy isn't about wealth; it's about giving what you can to a cause you believe in. To that end, then, any amount of money your family ultimately sets aside to help others is a welcome contribution to charitable organizations that routinely struggle to raise enough cash to meet the unending needs they serve.

Launch your fund by deciding how much your child will contribute every week or month, and then agree that Mom and

Dad (and any other family members who sign on) will match that sum either one for one or even two for one. By the way, you might combine this with the Giving jar, mentioned as part of the four-jar method of budgeting. As the weeks and months pass, you will see the wealth in the jar accumulate.

At regular intervals, come together as a family to decide how to distribute the money in the fund. How you define "regular interval" is up to you. Maybe you gather every month, maybe every quarter. At the very least you should do it every six months so that the giving happens frequently enough to impress the purpose and the process upon your child's consciousness. Equally important: You must bring your child into that process of selecting the charity that will benefit from the family's largesse. Don't let him be a bystander to the action. You want him intimately involved.

How to do that? Brainstorm ideas with your child. Ask what he cares about. You might be surprised at how thoughtful your child can be. A child who saw a grandparent suffer with dementia might want to help fund Alzheimer's research, or might want to spend time visiting with seniors at a local retirement home. Children often want to help other children who are disabled, disadvantaged or alone. They want to help animals. They are increasingly aware of environmental issues through school and even the TV shows they watch. Kids won't likely know charities associated with the causes they care about— though sometimes they will—so you will either need to offer suggestions of charities you know that fit the needs, or you will need to spend time together researching the charities that serve a particular cause.

Once you have a list of a few causes that fit your child's philanthropic interests, incorporate them into the family-charity fund. This first time the family gathers to donate money, allocate some or all of it to one of the choices on your child's list of charities. This way you're showing your child all the pieces coming together—from thinking about the causes that matter, to researching the charitable options that exist, to donating the time and money.

Ultimately, though, there are many ways the family can select a charity to support. Each family member can research and make a pitch for a worthy charity, and then the family as a whole votes on which one to support. Or, you can rotate between the charities each family member wants to support so that this time Mom's charity gets the money, while next it's your child's charity, and the time after that it's Dad's choice. Or, toss all the causes into a hat and pick the winner by luck of the draw. In short, there's no end to the creative ways you might use to determine how to donate the money your family earmarks for philanthropy.

The cause needn't be local, either. Gobs of overseas organizations need help with everything from caring for children in an orphanage to building a local school to helping with scientific projects. One option: a "volunteer vacation," in which you travel to a foreign country and spend most of your time in charitable work, and some of your time as a tourist getting to know the country, the people, their culture. Most organizations will allow children as young as 12 to participate, so long as they are accompanied by an adult guardian, such as a parent or grandparent. Scan the Web and you'll find a variety of organizations that arrange volunteer vacations in places as disparate as Ghana, Ecuador or the Cook Islands. Two well-regarded organizations that put together these types of vacations are Cross-Cultural Solutions (www.crossculturalsolutions.org) and Global Volunteers (www.globalvolunteers.org).

Volunteer vacations are a more expensive road to philan-thropy, given the travel costs, but they can open your child's eyes and mind to the wider world and also be one of the most amazing experiences your family will share.

Older Kids: Cash Poor, Ideal Rich

If nothing else, teenagers are both energetic and idealistic—a combination perfect for charitable causes because, while teens don't always have a ton of money, they do have an abundance of time and energy to devote to a particular need that resonates with them. Indeed, numerous examples exist of teens—some just preteens as young as 12—who start their own charity to serve a clear need they saw in their community or across bor-ders in other states or other countries.

Of course, the vast majority of kids aren't going to do that. Reflect on your own days as a teenager . . . you were groping for an identity to define the reflection you saw in the mirror. Thus, with most kids, finding the cause they want to support will take a little time.

In terms of charity, that means teens will likely try on vari-ous philanthropic causes, just like they try on various types of attire, looking for something that meshes with who they are or who they want to be. They might even support Mom and Dad's causes early on because doing so is, if nothing else, a conve-nient starting point.

Don't be surprised, though, if your cause célèbre is a bit passé to your child after a while. And don't be offended. More-over, as mentioned earlier, don't overreact if your teen finds a cause that runs counter to your own beliefs. Teens naturally seek a level of independence as they're growing into young adults, and your charitable leanings might not address their own desires. Or, it might be that they want to join forces with friends and schoolmates pushing a different agenda.

All of that is okay, though. You're not aiming to build a philanthropic doppelgänger. Your goal is so much simpler: building a caring human being who willingly devotes time, energy and resources to the betterment of the local and global community.

Kids & Money Rule #12: If a child's charitable interests lie outside your special interests, so be it.

That rule, however, doesn't mean you can let your child pull away from any family-charity fund or any family-charity rituals. Keeping the family active in the name of charity maintains a unity and a consistency that all kids benefit from. You might, however, consider allocating part of the fund's resources to your child's charity du jour as a show of togetherness. Maybe offer to use some of the family-charity fund money to match whatever money your child has saved or raised for a particular cause.

If your teen isn't into charitable giving but you want to encourage philanthropy, there are a couple of ways to effect that.

For birthday and holiday gifts skip the gift cards to the local mall and instead consider giving your teenager a "giving card"—a gift card that allows your child to donate to any of a variety of charities. You can find these giving cards all over the internet, at sites such as CharityNavigator.org and Global-Giving.com. Not to single out GlobalGiving for any specific reason, but it allows philanthropic cardholders to select from a few hundred charitable organizations that undertake activities ranging from funding the educational needs of children in developing nations to saving orangutans from extinction. Effectively, you're donating the money, but you're putting the choice of where the money goes into your child's hand, engaging them in the process of thinking beyond themselves about what they consider important in the wider world.

Finally, a reminder of a crucial thought from earlier in this chapter that kids need to understand: Philanthropy isn't about how much money you have or how much money you give. It's about giving what you can to a cause you believe in.

Ultimately, philanthropy is about your own personal financial situation, and it's part of the balancing act between spending, saving and giving. Kids need to learn, first, that to give means that first they have to save. That way they will have something to give in the first place. Then, they should also understand that giving means they're unable to spend and save as much as they otherwise might, and that this in itself is part of the charitable heart. In other words, you're depriving yourself of some value, some fun or even some financial security so that others might have a slightly more comfortable path through life.

That's the ultimate message you want your kids to grasp, and to one day apply to their own lives as adults.

Learning

SAVING FOR THE DIPLOMA

I started this book with a chapter on preparing yourself for the costs of raising a child. I'm ending it with a chapter on preparing yourself for the cost of educating that child, generally the last official act of financial support parents provide to their kids—assuming, of course, your child doesn't end up living at home for years after college. But that's an entirely different book.

Too often, parents freak out about the costs of college. There's little wonder why; the media routinely report in sometimes hyperbolic terms just how expensive college is, highlighting just how rapidly tuition is increasing annually. To make matters worse, they warn that financial aid is harder to obtain, and throw around numbers that make the cost of an education sound more like the gross domestic product of a small country or the down payment on a nice house.

To be fair, college can be a costly endeavor for families. The average price tag is more than $14,300 for a year's

tuition, fees and room and board at a four-year public insti-
tution for the 2008–09 school year, according to the College
Board, which tracks such data. At private schools, the annual
tally tops $34,100. Those are, no doubt, big—BIG—numbers
to many, many families.

But they are numbers that are half-truths at best.

Many families will never have to pay that kind of money
to send their kids to university. Numerous state schools are
dramatically less expensive, particularly for in-state students.
Many kids will live at home during their college years, sharply
reducing the necessary outlays. A number of states offer tax
incentives for families to stash dollars in particular types of
college savings accounts, which can help lower costs. And all
schools offer scholarships, grants and other forms of financial
aid that can trim costs dramatically. If you begin to save early,
the costs you ultimately confront will be much more manage-
able than you think. So don't start fretting just yet about having
to sell a lung to finance your child's enrollment at Harvard or
Michigan (one of the nation's priciest public schools) 18 years
from now.

Step back for a minute and recognize that all these reports
generally comment on how much the *average* college costs. How
many students do you know, though, who have attended the
University of Average? Before you begin thinking about saving
for college—or the seemingly impossible feat of doing so effectively—you have to figure out what you are saving for. By that,
I mean: Where is your child likely to go to college? Or, where
would you like your child to attend college? That answer is the
ending point in your quest to determine how much money you
ultimately need to save. And if you have an ending point, then
you can easily determine the path you need to get there. That

path is the amount of money you need to save each month to accumulate enough cash to afford college—or at least as much of it as you can comfortably afford or are willing to afford.

So, step one in any college savings plan is figuring out how much your school of choice is likely to cost when your child is ready to enroll. One of the best sources of data on tomorrow's college costs is found online at www.troweprice.com. T. Rowe Price is a large, well-respected financial services company, and its college-planning calculator provides cost projections for hundreds of specific colleges and junior colleges around the country. (You'll find the college-cost calculator if you click on the "How Much Will College Cost Me" in the College Planning link under "Planning & Research" in the section for Individual Investors. That could change over time as T. Rowe Price continually improves its website, so if the above directions are no longer accurate, hunt around for the calculator in the college-planning section.) Knowing real costs for the schools your child might one day attend means you're not working with an average that might be way off the mark. Instead, you'll have a better sense of the actual costs, and that can make your planning more accurate. Remember, though, that these are just projections; inflation could run higher or lower than expected and that would change the final number, possibly materially. But you have to work with some number, and this is about as realistic as you'll find.

Now, I know what you're thinking: How do I have any clue where my kid might go to college one day? You probably can't know that with any certainty. You might be thinking of some particular school (your alma mater, the dream school your parents couldn't afford, etc.), but who knows what will transpire between now and freshman orientation that might completely

upend your expectations. And that's OK. Again, you have to
start with some goal in mind, which is what this exercise is
really all about. If the goal changes along the way, well, then
you shift as best you can and keep moving forward.

But here's the real message, and it's our next rule:

Kids & Money Rule #13: Parents don't have to save every last
dime a child will need for college expenses. You only have to
save up to your ability or desire to pay.

I recognize that will strike some parents as odd or maybe
even untenable. After all, parents have been browbeaten into
believing they must sacrifice for the betterment of their children and that they must begin saving for college from Day One,
maybe even earlier. And, yes, to the degree you can, you should
put aside some money for your child's education. But in struggling to save the entire costs, parents often overlook three very
important points:

1. College costs often arrive during your peak earning
   years, allowing you to pay some or all of the costs from
   your income stream. Those future college costs might
   seem insurmountable from this distance, but just remember that your pay is likely to increase over time,
   putting those costs closer to your future income—even
   if only marginally closer.

2. Your child has the ability to earn scholarships or
   grants that can pay for college, or they can also take
   out student loans to pay those costs. Kids also can

work to pay the costs you can't afford, and they have an entire career to repay whatever debt they accumulate in pursuing a degree.

3. You do not have the ability to earn scholarships or grants to pay for retirement, and you don't want to have to work in retirement to afford your life.

That last point is, perhaps, the most significant in any conversation about college costs—though it's one that can make some parents cringe. I recognize that parents routinely feel a need to pay for college as a way to give their kids a leg up in life. If you can afford to do so, and still save for your own retirement, then by all means have at it. But the financial stress that many families feel stems from the dueling desires to fund both college and retirement when the monthly paychecks don't allow for that. In many cases, parental love and that feeling of being obligated to your children's betterment means you funnel more dollars into your child's future than your own, figuring you can start saving for retirement after the last of the college bills are paid.

Not such a wise plan, though. While college might cost between $25,000 and $100,000, depending on which school your kid attends, retirement will cost hundreds of thousands, and more likely a few million. Retirement is multiple times more expensive, and, thus, you aren't likely to have nearly enough time after your child graduates to save what you'll need to afford your golden years. Far smarter to save early and often for retirement, and then absorb as best you can the college costs as they arrive. And what you can't afford, your child can pay for through scholarships, loans, grants or their own labor.

Think about it in terms of this rule:

Kids & Money Rule #14: One of the greatest gifts you can give your child is your own financial self-sufficiency when you're old.

You might think that you are helping them by funding their college education, and, yes, to a certain degree you are. But in doing so you could be inadvertently burdening them when you're older and unable to fund your life in retirement. Do you really want to be calling your children and effectively begging for money to pay your bills because you've run out of money too soon? Or, if you're too proud to beg, do you really want to have to drastically scale back your life to the bare minimum when you'd rather be enjoying the freedom you've earned by punching a time clock for four decades or more? Those tens of thousands of dollars you shelled out for education—which, over time, would have grown into hundreds of thousands—are dollars you could instead be using to pay for your life in retirement. Your offspring will be far happier paying off college debt than paying off your bills. And here's the hook: You can help your children repay college debts *after* you retire. At that point you will have a much better idea of your costs, and you can allocate some of your savings to repaying those costs by gifting money to your children for that purpose. You will have effectively accomplished the same goal—paying for college—but you'll have done so from a position of financial strength after you have already built a nest egg big enough to support you in retirement. It's a smarter way to go.

But that doesn't mean you can't save a little along the way

to at least offer some level of financial aid when the tuition bills commence. So let's take a look at the savings options that you have, and the pros and cons of each.

College Savings Accounts

You have basically three choices: UGMA/UTMA accounts, Coverdell Educational Savings Accounts (formerly known as Education IRAs) and so-called 529 college savings plans.

UGMA/UTMA ACCOUNTS

I mentioned these in the chapter on Savings, but to refresh any cloudy memories, both of these are essentially the same thing: irrevocable gifts of cash or securities that you give to a minor. As custodial accounts, someone you designate—and that could be you—controls the assets for a named beneficiary who gains control of the account at the age of majority, typically 18 or 21, depending upon the jurisdiction.

UGMA/UTMA accounts are generally opened at brokerage firms, banks, mutual fund firms or trust companies. You can determine how the assets are invested, or you can hire a professional such as a stockbroker or trust-company money manager to do that work for you.

The greatest benefit of custodial accounts is their flexibility. You can own just about any asset your financial firm of choice allows—stocks, bonds, mutual funds, gold, silver, currency, commodities contracts, real estate, whatever. That gives you greater freedom to structure the underlying investments in whatever manner best suits your goals. Further, you can invest an unlimited amount of money in the account every year, meaning that everyone, grandparents, aunts, uncles or whoever, can contribute as much as they wish with no negative impacts on the account.

Several downsides exist, however. The most significant for many people is the "irrevocable" nature of the account. In other words, you can never reclaim the money. If your child—the account's beneficiary—decides to skip college altogether and pursue a career as a circus clown, or you decide for whatever reason you no longer want the beneficiary to have the money, well, you're out of luck. The beneficiary of a custodial account ultimately gains total control of the assets and can spend the money without any input from you.

Then there's the issue of taxes. The profits and income earned by assets in an UGMA/UTMA account are taxed every year, even if at the child's lower tax rate. But even tax-induced small reductions in an educational account can have large impacts years down the road, reducing the amount of money your beneficiary otherwise would have had by a substantial margin.

Finally, custodial accounts are not the friendliest when it comes to your child obtaining student aid to help pay for college—and every student should at least apply for some form of scholarship or grant. After all, free money to pay for college is the best money of all. When it comes to financial-aid calculations, universities typically consider half the value of a custodial account eligible to pay for college costs. That's a substantially larger percentage than is applied to parents if that same amount of money was held in their name instead.

Bottom Line: If there's any chance that your child might need to apply for student aid one day, UGMA/UTMA accounts generally aren't the best choice.

COVERDELL EDUCATIONAL SAVINGS ACCOUNT

If you understand an Individual Retirement Account, the so-called IRA I wrote about earlier in the book, then you'll understand a Coverdell. These accounts allow you to save tax-deferred money that you can withdraw and use, tax free, if it is spent on "qualified" educational expenses. This basically means you'll pay no taxes on profits or income as the account grows, and then you'll pay no taxes if the money is spent to cover the costs of qualified educational bills. (See the sidebar below for more on what constitutes "qualified.")

QUALIFIED EDUCATIONAL EXPENSES EXPLAINED

IRS Publication 970, found online at www.irs.gov (use the search box to find the specific publication), outlines exactly what expenses are considered "qualified." The list is quite short:

- Tuition and fees necessary to enroll.
- Expenses for special-needs services incurred by special-needs students.
- Books, supplies and equipment necessary to participate in classes. The IRS publication doesn't spell this out specifically, but "equipment" could mean a laptop computer if the school or a particular degree program requires students access the school's Internet site for various educational reasons.
- Room and board.

That's the extent of the list. Nothing else is covered.

Coverdell accounts are unique in that you can spend the money on private school costs that occur before college. So, for instance, a grandparent could fund a Coverdell when a grandchild is first born, and then parents could tap into the account to pay tuition at a private elementary, middle or high school. That benefit, however, could expire in 2010 if Congress doesn't act to prevent that.

If you ultimately withdraw the money for expenses other than education, or if the beneficiary doesn't attend college and instead spends the money on something else, then you will pay taxes on all the gains at your ordinary income-tax rate (typically among the highest rates), and you'll pay an additional penalty of 10% on those earnings. Moreover, Coverdells *must* be distributed by the time a beneficiary reaches the age of 30. If that doesn't happen, the account is forcibly distributed and the earnings are taxed as ordinary income and, again, penalized an additional 10%.

As with an IRA, you can invest a Coverdell in an endless variety of mutual funds and individual stocks and bonds, giving you a large selection of investments. Unlike an IRA, however, you cannot claim a deduction on your annual tax returns for your contributions.

Like UGMA and UTMA accounts, a Coverdell is a custodial account registered in the name—and under the Social Security number—of your beneficiary. That means, once again, that the beneficiary gains ultimate control of the account at some point. However, in some instances you can change the beneficiary, so long as all of the following are true:

- The trust agreement (the paperwork you sign that defines the account) allows for a beneficiary change, and not all do;

- The existing beneficiary is under the age of 30;
- The new beneficiary is under the age of 30;
- The new beneficiary is a member of the existing beneficiary's family.

Basically, this means that you can't decide to take back the money for yourself if you don't want your child to access the account, and that if you do want to change beneficiaries, the money in the account must go to your other children or the existing beneficiary's children, in other words, your grandchildren.

The biggest drawback: Coverdell accounts are limited to annual contributions of just $2,000 (and, again, if Congress doesn't act, the annual contribution limit could revert to its original amount of $500 after 2010). That's not per contributor, mind you, but per beneficiary. So you and the grandparents and the aunts and uncles combined can only contribute a grand total of $2,000 (or, possibly, $500) to the account each year. Oh, and you can't open a Coverdell and fund it to the max, and then have grandparents open a second account and fully fund that one as well. The annual contribution limit is spread across all Coverdell accounts in that beneficiary's name.

Certainly, any money put into college savings is good money, but $2,000, much less $500, may not be nearly enough to put much of a dent in your college bills if college costs continue rising as fast as they have been in recent years. You should also keep in mind that your ability to contribute to a Coverdell phases out for married wageearners at income levels between $190,000 and $220,000 in 2010. Phase-out for single wage earners occurs between $95,000 and $110,000. The Internal Revenue Service occasionally increases these limits, or Congress could increase the contribution limits, so pay attention to that if the Coverdell appeals to you.

Bottom Line: Assuming Congress keeps the status quo for Coverdell accounts, they can be beneficial if you intend to use the money to help pay for private school costs before college. But beyond that, other types of educational savings—such as the 529 plans detailed next—make much more sense for the average family. And if Congress doesn't act and Coverdells revert to a maximum $500-a-year contribution limit, then I would argue the accounts are near useless, since $500 compounded at an 8% annual rate over 18 years grows to less than $19,000 (the equivalent of about $11,000 in 2009). Given the costs of college in 2009 and the rate of growth in college tuition, that sum, even though it seems tidy, isn't likely to cover many educational expenses.

529 PLANS

These plans have become wildly popular among families saving for college. The plans afford the same tax breaks as a Coverdell—tax-deferred growth matched with tax-free withdrawals for qualified educational expenses—but they add other sweeteners that generally make them a smarter choice for most consumers.

First, when you save in a state-sponsored 529 plan, many states offer tax breaks beyond what you can write off on your federal tax return. Generally speaking, though, that applies only if you're saving in your home state's 529 plan. If you don't like that plan for whatever reason, you're free to invest in any plan in the country, regardless of your home address. Recognize, however, that if you do open a 529 plan outside your state of residence, you might not qualify for preferential treatment on your state taxes, though you will still get the preferred tax treatment at the federal level (tax-deferred growth and tax-free withdrawal for qualified expenses).

Second—and perhaps this actually should be first, depending on your priorities—you don't relinquish control of the account. These plans are held *in a parent's name*, not in the name of the ultimate beneficiary. That means your child can't one day grab the money you set aside for educational costs and fund a garage band. Moreover, you can easily name a new beneficiary if your original beneficiary doesn't need the money for college or doesn't go to college. In this case, the new beneficiary can be just about anyone: another child, a grandchild, a niece, a nephew . . . even yourself, if you decide you want to return to school one day.

You have two types of 529 plans to choose from:

With **prepaid plans** you literally prepay today for a set number of years of college courses or a predetermined number of college credits in the future. Basically you're locking in tomorrow's college costs today. In other words, if today you purchase a year's worth of college 18 years from now, your child is guaranteed to have those costs covered in the future, no matter how high college costs ultimately go. This is for an in-state public university, though. If your child ultimately opts to attend a private school either in or out of state, or decides to attend an out-of-state pubic university, the plan you contributed to will generally pay the average in-state tuition and fees for schools in the state of choice. However, the parents and the student are on the hook for costs that exceed that average.

Savings plans are the more popular choice. They operate much like a Coverdell, in that you periodically invest whatever sum of money you can afford, and the money is invested in whatever investment selection you choose. But unlike a Coverdell, you can save dramatically more money, generally about $250,000 per beneficiary, either in small contributions over time or in one or more larger, lump-sum payments. Also different, the plans need not be distributed by a certain age, allowing you to roll assets from one generation to the next, if you wish.

As with the Coverdell, though, if you do not use the assets in a 529 plan for qualified college costs, then you will pay taxes at ordinary rates on the earnings and income the assets have generated, and you'll pay that additional 10% penalty as well.

The other drawback is that 529 plans are generally quite limited in their investment selections; you won't be able to choose between a wide variety of mutual funds or individual stocks and bonds. Instead, most 529 plans only offer a few investment options, typically built around mutual funds that are either age-based or risk-based in their approach to investing. That said, parents pressed for time or those who don't want to muck about with investment management might well see this as a big benefit.

Age-based funds, which have become very popular with parents, effectively ask this question: How old is your child? Answer that question, and the portfolio management is handled for you by the investment firm.

The younger the child, the more aggressively the funds are invested, recognizing that with many years to go before the college bills arrive, you want to invest for the maximum growth. As your child ages, the fund grows increasingly more conservative so that a bad spell in the stock market doesn't destroy the value of the account. The best part: You don't have to do a thing after making your initial designation; the fund company changes the portfolio's mix automatically as college enrollment draws nearer and nearer.

Risk-based funds, meanwhile, gauge your tolerance for risk. The riskier you are, the more aggressive the fund. The more conservative you are, the more conservative the fund's investments. You typically have to keep track of this yourself, though, remembering to adjust your tolerance level as your kid ages. If you invest aggressively early on and then forget to adjust your allocation as your child ages, you risk losing a huge chunk of the college account in a market meltdown. Likewise, invest too conservatively all along the way and you risk not accumulating nearly as much as you might have otherwise.

To summarize, here are the two key differences between prepaid and savings plans.

First: Prepaid plans are guaranteed to keep up with college-cost inflation, so that your child is guaranteed to receive as many years or as many credit hours as you originally paid for. Savings plans, meanwhile, will grow to whatever level the investments reach, and if that's enough to pay the costs, great; if not, you'll have to find a way to supplement the shortfall.

Second: The two types of plans have sharply different impacts on financial aid. College aid officers deem prepaid plans to be a "resource" for college costs specifically, and, thus, the balance of whatever need-based financial aid your child requires reduces by 100% of the account value. That can have a marked impact if you've only prepaid for a partial education. Savings plans, conversely, are seen as an "asset" of the parent, and federal financial aid formulas typically assume that a maximum of 5.64% of parental assets are eligible to pay for college costs. Thus, if you have a $20,000 account when your child applies for college, the entire sum in a prepaid plan is factored into your child's need for financial aid, while with a savings plan only $1,128 is factored into the calculations.

At one point, the tax advantages of 529 savings plans were set to expire at the end of 2010. However, that shadow no longer overhangs these accounts. In passing the Pension Protection Act of 2006, Congress did away with that sunset clause and now 529 plans and their tax-advantaged status have a permanent place in the world of college savings.

Bottom Line: For the vast bulk of American families, the 529 plan is the smartest approach to college savings. Though some might view the relative paucity of investment options as a weakness, others will see that fewer choices means less to fret about when trying to select between this fund and that fund.

The tax-free aspect makes them a better bet than UGMA and UTMA accounts, while the size of the contributions allowed makes it much easier for parents to save a considerably larger sum than is possible with Coverdell accounts.

Finally, the control parents retain over the account and the ability to change beneficiaries give 529 plans greater flexibility than the other options.

College Savings Credit Cards

One of the easiest ways to save for college is to use credit cards that offer a rebate on the everyday purchases you make. Those rebates ultimately flow directly into a 529 plan, and effectively mean that the items you buy to live your life—from groceries to restaurant meals to vacation expenses—help you pay for college. The two big players in this area are financial services giant Fidelity Investments and Upromise, owned by SLM Corp., the big student loan firm known as Sallie Mae.

With Upromise, for instance, you can earn between 1% and

25% on the items you purchase online through the Upromise site. These are nationally known retailers such as Amazon. com, Wal-Mart, Target, Williams-Sonoma and McDonald's. Upromise also offers a credit card for which you earn back at least 1% of your net retail purchases. So if your monthly credit card bill is $1,000, Upromise dumps at minimum $10 into your college savings account. The dollars that land in your account are then periodically swept into a mutual fund. Just as I mentioned several pages back with the investment options inside a 529 plan, these funds are generally managed based on age or risk tolerance. You have some choice in which fund you want the money to go into, but the selections are exceedingly limited—just a select few funds. You can find out more about each program at www.upromise.com and www.fidelity.com (search for "college rewards").

Now you might not think that picking up 1% for buying a $5 carton of milk, or five cents, is really going to help you reach your savings goal. Admittedly, even if you received 5% back on every purchase—and you won't—you'd have to spend about $1.14 million on your credit card to pay for four years of college at the average cost of $14,300 per year that I mentioned at the start of this chapter. That equals out to about $63,555 a year for 18 years, and you'll need to take into account the annual cap that many of these cards impose. All of this excludes investment returns on the invested money, which would clearly shrink the amount of spending you'd ultimately have to do, but the message is nevertheless the same; the average family isn't likely to realistically spend enough to afford college simply through one of these plans.

However, when you pool together all the purchases you make in a given year, you'll be surprised at how the dollars can add up. The money that does accrue can be enough to afford part of your child's tuition, some room and board expenses or several semesters' worth of books and supplies. And while I bemoan the small savings that accumulate in a Coverdell account, here the small sum is a different story: We're talking free money. You're earning cash for buying items you would have otherwise purchased anyway, so these programs can be a pretty useful two-for-one deal.

Recognizing that spending on groceries and gasoline alone won't create a huge stash of college cash, these credit card programs also let you contribute an additional amount of money on a monthly or quarterly basis, if you wish, so that you can build your account balance. These regular monthly or quarterly investments are set up so that they're automatically drawn out of your checking or savings account, saving you the hassle of having to remember to send in the additional cash.

Financial Aid

Tons of books are available on financial aid, so I'm not going to spend a great deal of time explaining all the intricacies. But as long as we're talking about college and how you're going to afford it, you need to know about the financial aid system so that you can begin to consider the possibilities that exist.

Too many parents and college-bound kids rule out a particular school because the cost is, in theory, just too much. You hear names like Harvard, Yale and Duke and you might think "way too pricey for my family." Actually, they might not be. Assuming that a certain school is too expensive, and reflexively ruling it out based on the cost, is one of the biggest mistakes parents make. The amount of aid your child might qualify for at a school is relative to the cost of attending that particular school. So, the pricier the school, the larger the amount of money your child ultimately could receive.

It works like this: The aid available to your child equals the cost of attending college minus your family's "expected contribution," which is the sum of money the federal student aid process determines your family can afford. Whatever remains is your child's "demonstrated need," the amount of money that college aid officers help you try to accumulate through grants, work-study programs, scholarships, and the like.

Certainly, I'm not implying your child will necessarily receive the total amount needed. She very well might, or she might receive less. The point, however, is that a higher sticker price does not automatically mean you have to pay more out of pocket. It just means your kids are potentially eligible for a greater level of aid.

As for that aid, it basically comes from three sources: grants and scholarships, loans, and the Federal Work-Study Program. Here's what you need to know about each:

Grants and Scholarships: This is the best money of all when it comes to paying for college, because this is free money. With grants and scholarships, you don't have to repay anything. They're awarded by a variety of organizations, from governments and companies to charities, foundations, fraternal orders and the universities themselves, among others.

Generally speaking, scholarships are merit based, rather than being based on a family's financial need. That means your student-to-be must demonstrate some sort of academic, artistic or athletic prowess, or some level of civic leadership. In one of the more interesting exceptions to that rule, the Henkel Corp., in Avon, Ohio, annually awards a $5,000 scholarship to the high school couple that designs and wears the most creative prom attire fashioned entirely from the company's Duck brand duct tape. Websites such as www.fastweb.com and www.collegeanswer.com both provide comprehensive lists of millions of scholarships worth billions of dollars annually. Yes, billions. And you'd be surprised how much of that money isn't awarded each year because of lack of applicants.

Check with the university your child is interested in attending to find out what grants and scholarships might be available. Check, too, with the specific academic department where your child will enroll. At many schools, the various departments—such as chemistry, engineering, mathematics—distribute their own scholarships to students pursuing a particular degree.

Meanwhile, high school juniors and seniors should meet with guidance counselors, who annually receive hundreds of local scholarship notices that universities typically won't know about. These are generally small, frequently no more than $500 or $1,000, though some can be larger. Apply for as many as your children are eligible for. And here's a hint: Keep all your application material, such as required essays. With some creativity, you can recycle those to ease some of the paperwork burden inherent in pursuing multiple scholarships or grants.

One of the largest grants programs in the country is the federal government–provided Pell Grant, which dishes out billions of dollars annually to tens of millions of students. The grants—which generally total about $2,500 per recipient—are based solely on financial need, as determined by the Free Application for Federal Student Aid, the so-called FAFSA form. That form is available online at www.fafsa.ed.gov. Colleges use this form to determine eligibility for federal, state and university scholarships and grants. You want to submit the FAFSA form to your child's selected colleges as early in the calendar year as possible. Schools start to dole out aid dollars for the approaching fall academic year early in the spring, so you want your FAFSA form in the aid office in January or February.

NOT-SO-FREE FAFSA

When college finally arrives and you start trolling the Internet for aid, you are almost certain to stumble upon companies that, for a fee of a few hundred dollars, guarantee they can find aid dollars for your child. That's a pretty enticing deal . . . *guaranteed* aid dollars.

Don't bite. It's a scam.

These companies collect a variety of family and financial information from you, dump it into a FAFSA form and obtain for you a $1,000 loan that you could have secured yourself for free with the same paperwork.

In fact, with all the free assistance available from high school guidance counselors, university aid offices and free Internet searches, there's no need to pay for help. Do so and you're just wasting dollars you could spend on college costs directly.

Loans: If scholarships and grants and other programs don't corral enough cash to cover college costs, you can always borrow. The federal government and a variety of private lenders offer college-loan programs.

The federal Stafford Loan is the largest program of all, dispensing tens of billions of dollars annually in student aid. Two types of Stafford Loans are available:

- *Subsidized*: Here, the federal government pays the interest while the student is in school, as well as for the first six months after graduation and, if necessary, a period of deferment. Subsidized loans are awarded based solely on financial need, as determined by the FAFSA form. The interest rate that the government charges is variable.
- *Unsubsidized:* These are available to any student, regardless of financial need. Students are responsible for interest payments from the outset, though they can allow the interest to accrue and roll into the principal while pursuing a degree. The interest rate is also variable.

How much money a student is eligible for from a Stafford Loan depends on the student's academic year (freshman, sophomore, etc.), whether the student is considered dependent on parents or is independent, and whether the student is in undergraduate or graduate school. For a handy breakdown of how much a student is eligible for (and these numbers change, so it's a bit pointless to print out-of-date data here), visit the federal student aid website at www.studentaid.ed.gov. In fact, you'll find information on all federal loan and grant programs at that website.

Parents also have a federal loan option to help pay for a child's college costs—the Parent Loans for Undergraduate Students, or PLUS loans. Parents can borrow up to the total cost of attendance, minus whatever aid the student receives. There are no asset or income limits, though you must pass a credit check that shows you're not more than 90 days past due on any other debt obligations. As such, if you find that a PLUS loan is helpful, spend several months cleaning up your credit by getting current on all your accounts before applying.

Private lenders are also big players in the college loan market, led by Wells Fargo, Bank of America and SLM Corp's Sallie Mae. Smaller, local banks also make education loans. With private lenders, though, be prepared to pay higher interest rates. You're also likely to be subject to more rigorous underwriting standards, meaning a lender is going to pull apart your financial life to determine if you're worthy of the loan.

Work-Study: This is a federally funded, needs-based program in which students work part-time while they're in school to pay for the costs of their degree. Jobs are typically on campus, though in some situations the jobs might be off campus, often with a local community-service program or public agency. Pay ranges between minimum wage and $10 or $12 an hour, depending upon skills necessary for the job. Earnings cannot exceed the financial need determined by the FAFSA form—so kids aren't going to earn enough to pay for college and then have spending money for a swank condo off campus and beer money for the weekend.

One final thought: If you or your child don't want to take on a loan, and scholarships and grants aren't enough to pay for tuition, many universities offer a payment plan. For a small fee, generally less than $100, schools will offer you an interest-free payment schedule that allows you to pay that year's unfunded costs over 10 or 12 months. Such an arrangement can help parents more easily match college expenses to their monthly income.

DEMYSTIFYING THE FEDERAL FINANCIAL AID FORMULA
· · · · · · · ·

At its core, the federal formula for determining how much aid a student is eligible for is based on the notion that parents and students bear some responsibility to pay to whatever extent they're able. That extent is called your Expected Family Contribution, or EFC.

In coming to the EFC, the formula takes into account the assets and income of parents and the student. The formula regards as available to pay college costs the following:

- 35% of a student's assets
- 50% of a student's income
- 2.6% to 5.6% of parents' assets
- 22% to 47% of parents' income

The formula also takes into account the oldest parent's age. The older that parent is, the larger the amount of assets that are automatically sheltered from the calculation. It does this because the formula recognizes that parents have other costly expenses to save for, namely retirement. As such, assets in retirement plans are excluded from the formula. So, too, is the value of a primary residence.

The upshot is that assets earmarked for college are typically best held in the name of the parents, since that will generally result in a student being eligible for a greater amount of financial aid. The only time that's not the case is when Mom and Dad have a vast amount of assets held outside of retirement accounts, in which case 5.6% of their assets may well exceed 50% of the child's assets.

This is another reason why it pays to save for retirement before college; you're maximizing not just your retirement savings, but enhancing your child's chances of earning as much financial aid as possible.

Just Say No: Closing the Pocketbook for Good

The final financial lesson parents much teach their children is often the hardest. So let's just get the last Kids & Money rule on the table immediately:

Kids & Money Rule #15: At some point you have to tell your kids that the Bank of Mom & Dad is officially closed.

I say this is one of the hardest lessons to teach because, as a parent, it often pulls at your heartstrings. The little five-year-old who looked up to you as though you were a superhero, the one who, with a delirious smile on his face, ran to you every afternoon when you walked in the door, the one who, when you were stretched out on the couch, crawled on top of your stomach to lay and watch TV with you . . . that little kid becomes an adult, and, despite that fact, you will be consumed by overpowering urges to do anything you can to help that little kid you still see inside your grown child.

Only you shouldn't. And that's what hurts.

Nevertheless, creating financially self-sufficient children requires that you close your pocketbook for good at some point, that you shutter the ATM they've siphoned for so many years. If you don't, if you allow your children to routinely run home—literally or metaphorically—for financial help every time they need money, their financial troubles will forever be your burden. They will never learn to manage their own financial affairs because they know someone (you) will always step in to bail them out of a bad situation. What's worse is that you are allowing your kids to consume the cash you'll need for your own retirement one day, and when you're gone you will leave behind adults who are lost financially, and who will find no one to replace you and your perennially open wallet.

Many kids will naturally wean themselves off your finances once they leave college and find jobs and begin living their own adult lives. Some will wean themselves while they're in college, earning their own money even as they earn their degree. Others, not so much. They're so accustomed to the easy access they have to your money that they can't pull away. That's particularly true after college, when your offspring are earning modest wages in their first job, and the lifestyle they once knew at home falls sharply.

Of course, recent college grads aren't the only culprits. Adults well into their thirties and forties and beyond regularly ask parents for a handout. Many of these creatively named "boomerang kids" move back home with their parents, creating the great potential for both emotional and financial fallout.

Whatever the case and regardless of your boomerang child's age, Mom and Dad cannot be responsible for supporting an able-bodied child's life or lifestyle forever. While there's nothing wrong with helping your offspring get on their feet, there's a great deal wrong with allowing those kids to continue draining your finances when they are capable of paying their own way through life.

Thus, whether it's helping a grown child living away from home, or opening your house to a boomerang kid, Mom, Dad and child must come together and determine the ground rules of this financial arrangement. No one right answer exists because all families and all situations are different. The answer that works for you will be based largely on your personal set of values and the degree to which your finances can absorb the hit. Indeed, before you ever sit down with your child to discuss what you're willing to provide, spend some time with a local financial planner to assess how much you can afford to help without drastically impacting your ability to provide for your own financial needs in retirement.

After you have that figured out, and after you and your partner have spent time privately discussing the rule you two want to impose on the situation, call a meeting with your child to talk about what level of help he needs, what level of help you can offer, and a timeline for ending the arrangement at some point. An outcome that makes everyone happy depends entirely on open, clear communication and a well-defined plan of attack. Without that, you risk a temporary arrangement becoming a quasipermanent lifestyle that begets anger, frustration and discord.

This meeting should be wide-ranging and might even result in a written contract so that everyone involved knows precisely the ground rules that are in place. In no particular order, the key issues to hash out are:

- **Rent:** You probably shouldn't charge market rent; after all, if your child could afford to pay the market rate he probably wouldn't be seeking help. But you should charge something, even if it's just $100 a month. That puts the onus on your offspring to be responsible for earning money, a particular need among recent college grads, who often want to hold out for the perfect job or one that pays an unreasonable amount of money. What you don't tell your kids is that you're not actually putting their payment toward the rent or mortgage you have to pay, but that you are instead setting that money aside in a separate bank account that you will turn over to your child one day when she's back on her feet and moving out for good. This will provide that extra financial cushion that can make the transition into her new life easier.

- **The Plan of Attack:** How long is this financial arrangement expected to last? Assuming there's a need to search for a job, what is your child's job-search strategy? How much money does your child need to save before moving out again, how and where is that money being saved, and will the child share monthly or quarterly bank statements to show progress in that direction?

- **Financial Contribution:** How much money can your child contribute to the family's needs? Another person back under your roof necessarily increases your family's cost for everything from electricity to food to water. You might even have to change your homeowner's insurance policy to cover your child's possessions in your house or in your garage, and you might need to alter your auto coverage if your child will be using a family car to get around town. Do not provide these for free when your offspring is capable of earning an income to help cover those costs. Determine how much he should contribute monthly.

- **Gift or Loan:** Is the money you and your spouse are spending effectively a gift for which you don't expect repayment? Or is all or part of it a loan, which you do expect your child to repay once she's supporting herself?

- **The Limit in Time and Dollars:** How long are you, the parent, willing to provide assistance, or are you opening your home for an unlimited period? How much money are you willing to contribute to your kid's financial needs, either on a monthly basis or in aggregate?

- **Debt Restructuring:** Is your child's financial incapacity caused by burdensome debt (credit cards, auto loans, school loans, etc.)? If so, detail the degree you are willing to help them out. Do not pay off the debt completely, otherwise no lesson will be learned. Instead, consider matching the debt-reduction efforts of your child. And be sure to insist that this is a one-time offer, that if debt gets out of hand again, you're not stepping in. Also, if you're helping pay off credit card debt, insist that the balance not increase, which means you have access to credit card statements to verify for yourself that your rule is being followed.

- **Work in Kind:** If your child has no job and cannot afford to pay rent or other costs immediately, determine what services and chores he can perform regularly around the house. If you pay a lawn service to tend to your yard and landscaping, maybe your boomerang son can take on those duties to save you that monthly cost.

- **What Parents Will Pay For:** Be specific about the items you will help pay for, be it the matching payments for debt reduction or rent, if your child continues to live on her own. But don't give your child the cash to make those payments. Instead, make them yourself. This way you are absolutely certain your money is paying for what you intended. Maybe your daughter isn't the type to redirect your help into other expenses, but by paying the costs yourself you are mitigating a potential sore spot before it ever develops.

Again, I stress, put all of this in writing. Kids who return home often revert to their childhood ways because they're back at home with Mom and Dad, and they might presume that the same rules apply today as applied when they were just kids. That's where the misunderstandings roost. A contract will negate those worries.

And if you find after your boomerang child has returned that the resulting friction is causing unnecessary stress within the family, and you cannot seem to gain control over it, you need the assistance of a family therapist who can help improve the situation. You can find a local therapist by searching online at the American Association of Marriage and Family Therapy (www.aamft.org).

Finally, when the predetermined time arrives for the arrangement to end, pull the plug, as painful as that might be for both you and your child. You might offer a six-month reminder that the cutoff is coming, but be cautious in extending the date, unless extraordinary events necessitate an extension. In providing more time, absent a clear and obvious reason, you are establishing that you don't really mean what you say. Your kid will know that, just like when he was much younger, a few sad, puppy-dog looks and a bit of begging will manipulate you into keeping the money flowing.

In the end, boomerang kids can be a joy to have around. Such a situation gives parents more time with their children and can strengthen the bonds at a time when your child is more mature than those final, hormone-driven teenage years that brought on all those gray hairs. Boomerang kids can be a help around the house. They can provide Mom and Dad with a sense of security and well-being, and an overwhelming sense of happiness.

But just make sure everyone is on the same page, that you don't feel taken advantage of, and that your child is diligently working toward the goals each of you has established. And when the time comes, cut the cord and don't look back. Otherwise your boomerang will return and hit your finances hard without benefiting his.

CONCLUSION

· · · · · · · · · · · · · · · · · ·

Teaching kids *anything* about life and growing up often feels about as productive as teaching a pig to sing: The effort all too often seems a waste of your time . . . and the pig's.

But then one day you hear something that you'll swear is music to your ears and you'll realize all your words weren't in vain. That day happened for me driving back from one of my son's soccer games. He was 12 at the time and a teammate was with us. A flashy, expensive Italian sports car pulled up alongside of us on the freeway and the teammate said, "Wow, that guy's rich."

My son, engrossed in a handheld video game at that moment, looked up to glance at the roadster and reflexively replied, "It's not how much money you spend that makes you rich. You don't know; that guy might have spent all his money just to buy that car and he has nothing else. So he might not be rich at all."

The messages of this book, it turns out, do sink in.

My son had heard my messages through the years. Here

he was casually correcting a teammate about what is and isn't the definition of wealth, barely even having to think about what he was saying. The words were coming out effortlessly. In the driver's seat, I was beaming—if not slightly amazed to hear his commentary—because more important than the message to his teammate was the underlying message to me: Mom and Dad really can make a difference when they set out to instill a bit of financial wisdom in their children.

Through the years, you will undoubtedly feel, as I much too frequently did; that you're wasting your breath for all the good you're doing your son. Unless we were engaged in conversations he initiated about his allowance or how he might afford a video game, he routinely seemed disinterested, disengaged or distracted whenever I tried to talk about money with him. Yet clearly some part of his brain was absorbing the information.

Thus, no matter your impression, keep on hammering away at those lessons you want your kids to learn. Your words will ultimately make a dent.

Kids have an infinite ability to hear what we parents say even in those moments we're convinced they're off in their own world, not paying attention to a word we're saying. And, in practice, the concept you're pushing might not sink in the first time. Or the third time. Or the eighth time. But there will come a moment when you say what you need to say for the umpteenth time, and the way you phrase your comment or the mood of the moment or the experience your child just had will cause your lesson, almost miraculously, to suddenly resonate.

Of course, you might not know it at that moment because, well, life's not a cartoon and you don't actually see the lightbulb brighten above your child's head. You will know it, though, when you see your lessons in action or, as I did, hear your lessons repeated by your child trying to teach a sibling or a friend.

This observation points to one of the overriding messages of this book: Begin the lessons early and keep at it. Kids are far more impressionable when they're younger and much less likely to have any sort of experiences outside the family cocoon that could shape their thinking before you do. That's not to say you can't erase the habits or beliefs they pick up—just that it could be more troublesome. By the time kids are hardened teenagers, your messages won't resonate nearly as strongly. Plus, you won't have many years to cram in all the lessons you want to instill. Of course, don't give up trying. Even with older kids you have some time remaining; use that time to teach the financial lessons that you deem the most critical.

To end this book, then, I'm not going to offer up some feel-good, daytime talk–show pabulum. For the truth is that being a parent is a dirty—not to mention thankless and frustrating—job at times. Also, I'm not going to pretend that money lessons are the most important lessons you'll teach your kids. Clearly, that's not the case; so many of the issues you need to deal with as a parent are so much more important.

Nevertheless, money remains a significant life skill. Too many adults today lack a fundamental understanding of personal finance themselves, a fact blindingly evident in 2007 and 2008 when the housing market crumbled under the weight of magical mortgages that had seduced financially ill-prepared home buyers into believing they could buy homes they couldn't afford. Part of that fault lies with a banking system that hawked predatory mortgages onto consumers, but those consumers wouldn't have accepted the onerous probabilities inherent in those too-good-to-be-true mortgages if they had any basic understanding of what they were doing. Sadly, much of this might have been avoided if their own parents—or even the educational system—had done a better job teaching their kids about matters of the wallet.

Ultimately, this book's aim isn't to help you mold children who only care about financial riches and the pursuit of wealth. Instead, its two-fold purpose is far less materialistic:

Goal #1: To help you prepare financially for bringing a child into your life, so that you can better manage the pre-arrival costs; determine the feasibility of becoming a one-income family if you decide stay-at-home parenting is your goal; and fit into the family budget all the clothes and doctor visits and school supplies and dance classes and sports equipment and toys—and chicken nuggets—without creating financial hardship. By working on your own finances first, you mitigate many of the monetary stresses that gnaw at relationships and that kids, in turn, can't help but sense.

You don't want that. When kids constantly sense that money is a source of woe—that even Mom and Dad, whom kids often assume are almost flawless, can't handle the pressure—they can't help but question how it is they can be expected to do any better.

Goal #2: To help you raise children who grow into adults who are financially aware and who are comfortable managing the various aspects of money, whether spending, saving, investing or giving back.

Maybe your child does accumulate financial riches. Maybe not. But the true measure of your success in this endeavor is that your child, as an adult, never struggles to understand the basics of personal finance. That will prove a far greater legacy than any inheritance you might one day leave behind.

Piggybanking Through the Years

There's lots of commentary in this book pointing out when kids are generally ready for a particular lesson, or when parents should begin pursuing something financially for their children. All that information can get blurred over the course of roughly 220 pages.

So, just as I proffered a cheatsheet at the start of this book to help parents locate the various Kids & Money rules scattered throughout, this is a cheatsheet of the various milestones. Certainly, I encourage you to read—or reread—the pertinent chapters, but I recognize that a quick-reference guide can help parents determine what milestones they should be dealing with at the moment, and which ones are upcoming that they should be thinking about and preparing for soon.

BEFORE BABY

Several months prior to a planned pregnancy, or when you find out unexpectedly you are pregnant:

- Budget for the one-time items you need and spread those expenses across several months, though you can expect to receive some as gifts.

DURING PREGNANCY:

- Prepare your budget for the ongoing expenses so that you can make the necessary spending adjustments now to afford the costs you will face.
- Determine how you structure a one-income family, if stay-at-home parenting is your family's goal.

BABY'S FIRST MONTHS

1 to 3 months:

- Get a life insurance checkup—or get life insurance!—to ensure that your child is cared for in the event something happens to you, your partner, or both of you. Once you have a child, you must have life insurance.

1 month to 1 year:

- Establish a college savings plan of some sort, such as a 529. It's never too soon to start saving for the expense you will ultimately face in 18 years.

AGES 1 TO 5

1 year old:

- Open your child's first savings account at the bank. Your child won't interact with it for a few years, but use it to stash birthday and holiday checks that arrive from friends and relatives.
- Fund an annuity for your child with a minimum investment, usually $5,000. Sixty-seven years later, when your child retires, your foresight will make your child's retirement easier and more memorable.

4 to 5 years old:

- Consider paying their first allowance. Rather than money, employ a system based on stickers or points tradable for items like a movie or dinner out with Mom and Dad.
- Baby's first piggybank.

5 years old:

- Establish age-appropriate chores, such as picking up toys in the house, but do not offer payment for these. Encourage age-appropriate bonus chores that will earn extra stickers or bonus points.

Ages 5 and above:

- Teach kids about "wants" and "needs" by having them help you determine the week's grocery list and label each item as either a want or a need.

AGES 6 TO 11

Age 6:

- Pay a weekly allowance based on real dollars, assuming your child can differentiate between various coins and bills and demonstrates an interest in having a bit of money to spend at the store.
- Begin the Four-Jar Budget when you begin paying an allowance of real money.
- Institute the save-and-match strategy, encouraging savings by offering to match some portion of the money your child saves.
- Introduce your child to that savings account you started years ago.

Age 6 or 7:

- Add a rate-of-return feature to the savings your child amasses in a piggybank or in the Savings jar to teach kids how compound interest can increase your savings.

- Begin instilling charitable ways by having kids put aside 10% to 15% of their allowance for charity, and by donating time together as child and parent for charitable causes, particularly those that resonate with kids.

Ages 6 and beyond:

- Increase the chore requirements with age, again absent any pay. Continue to encourage bonus chores, though this time tied to extra income.

Ages 7 and beyond:

- Play the "Dollar or a Soda?" game with your children when eating at a restaurant to help teach delayed gratification.

Ages 8 to 10:

- Introduce concepts of investing, even if only by routinely making note of publicly traded companies you own when passing a store or sign or whatever it is that denotes that particular company.

Ages 9 to 11:

- Open your child's first brokerage account.

Ages 10 to 11:

- Begin a family charity fund in which all members of the family contribute to a charity that the family decides to support. At age 10 and above, consider volunteer vacations.

Age 11 or 12:

- Alter allowance payment schedule, moving from once a week to once a month to get kids accustomed to managing their money across a longer period of time.

AGES 12 TO 16

Ages 12 and above:

- Allot kids enough money to pay for middle school supplies, and put them in charge of selecting and buying various needs and wants, but only within the limits of the money allotted.
- Introduce the concept of debt by drawing up a formal loan agreement when kids want to "borrow" money, a childhood euphemism for "give me money."
- Allow teens to determine their own charitable causes to support, even if those clash with your charitable leanings.

Ages 12 to 15:

- Encourage kids to earn spending money by raking leaves, babysitting, teaching skateboard, or doing whatever they enjoy for which they might earn a fee.

Ages 12 to 16:

- Establish 401(K)ids Plan to teach the concept of investing for retirement.
- Work on investment concepts with kids, like picking out stocks or mutual funds together. If you're picking stocks, focus on kid-friendly stocks that your child will instantly recognize.

Ages 14 to 15:

- Open child's first checking account.

Age 15 or 16:

- Time for a kid's first credit card, preferably with a built-in limit of just a few hundred dollars.

Age 16:

- Help your child locate a first job for which an employer offers a regular paycheck.

- Set up an Roth IRA (Individual Retirement Account) if your child is employed and earns what the IRS deems "reportable income."

Ages 16 to 18:
- Have your college-bound junior or senior meet with high school guidance counselors about scholarships and grants that are available for college. Begin applying.

AGES 17 TO 18

Age 17 (or high school junior):
- Alter allowance payment strategy again, moving from monthly payments to quarterly payments, or even payments covering an entire school semester, to teach kids to look into the immediate future to plan upcoming expenses as well as known, longer-range costs.

January of high school senior year:
- Fill out FAFSA form and submit to the colleges of your choice to begin pursuing the variety of financial aid options that are available.

DURING COLLEGE OR AFTER:
- Begin the process of cutting the cord financially.

Acknowledgments

. . . .

My son, Zach, and my daughter, Nicole, helped make this book possible because through them and their exploits I have learned so much about the joys, challenges and frustrations of parenthood and piggybanks. I love you both immensely.

INDEX

· · · · · · · · · ·

Note: Page numbers followed by a "t" refer to text boxes.